Culinary Futures

Lee Hernandez's Food Technology

Mei Moreno

ISBN: 9781779666123
Imprint: Press for Play Books
Copyright © 2024 Mei Moreno.
All Rights Reserved.

Contents

Introduction

The Future of Food

Exploring the possibilities

The future of food is not merely a reflection of current culinary trends; it is a canvas upon which innovation, technology, and sustainability are painted. As we delve into the myriad possibilities that lie ahead, we must consider the intersection of food science, consumer preferences, and the pressing global challenges that demand creative solutions. This section aims to explore these possibilities, highlighting the theoretical frameworks, existing problems, and real-world examples that shape the landscape of culinary innovation.

Theoretical Frameworks in Food Innovation

At the heart of culinary innovation lies a robust theoretical framework that encompasses various disciplines, including food science, nutrition, and technology. The integration of these fields is crucial for understanding how new food products can be developed to meet the needs of an ever-evolving society.

One prominent theory is the **Diffusion of Innovations** by Everett Rogers, which posits that the adoption of new ideas and technologies follows a predictable pattern. Innovations in food technology, such as plant-based meat alternatives or lab-grown proteins, exemplify this theory. The adoption curve can be broken down into five categories: innovators, early adopters, early majority, late majority, and laggards. Understanding where culinary innovations fall within this curve can help food technologists strategize their product launches and marketing efforts.

$$\text{Adoption Rate} = \frac{\text{Number of Adopters}}{\text{Total Population}} \times 100 \qquad (1)$$

1

This equation illustrates how the adoption rate can be quantified, allowing innovators to gauge the success of their culinary products in the market.

Identifying Problems in the Food System

Despite the advancements in food technology, significant challenges persist within the global food system. Issues such as food insecurity, environmental sustainability, and health concerns are pressing problems that require innovative solutions. For instance, the **Food Insecurity** Index highlights the alarming number of individuals who lack reliable access to sufficient food. According to the United Nations, approximately 690 million people were undernourished in 2019, a figure that has only worsened due to the COVID-19 pandemic.

$$\text{Food Insecurity Rate} = \frac{\text{Number of Food Insecure Individuals}}{\text{Total Population}} \times 100 \quad (2)$$

This equation can help policymakers and food innovators assess the scope of food insecurity within specific demographics, guiding targeted interventions.

Another critical issue is the environmental impact of food production. The food industry is responsible for approximately 25% of global greenhouse gas emissions. Innovations that promote sustainable practices, such as vertical farming and regenerative agriculture, are essential for mitigating this impact. For example, vertical farms utilize hydroponics and aeroponics to grow food in urban environments, minimizing land use and reducing transportation emissions.

Examples of Culinary Innovations

To illustrate the potential of food technology, we can examine several groundbreaking innovations that have emerged in recent years. One notable example is the development of **lab-grown meat**, which promises to address both ethical and environmental concerns associated with traditional meat production. Companies like *Memphis Meats* and *Impossible Foods* are at the forefront of this movement, utilizing cellular agriculture to create meat products without the need for livestock.

The process involves harvesting animal cells and cultivating them in a controlled environment, allowing for the production of meat that is virtually indistinguishable from conventionally raised meat. This innovation not only reduces the carbon footprint associated with animal agriculture but also addresses animal welfare concerns.

Carbon Footprint Reduction $=$ Traditional Meat Emissions $-$ Lab-Grown Meat Emissions

$$(3)$$

This equation can quantify the environmental benefits of lab-grown meat, making it an attractive option for environmentally conscious consumers.

Another exciting advancement is the use of **3D food printing**, which allows for the customization of food shapes, textures, and flavors. Companies like *Foodini* are pioneering this technology, enabling chefs to create intricate designs and personalized meals on demand. This innovation not only enhances the dining experience but also has the potential to reduce food waste by utilizing ingredients more efficiently.

The Role of Consumer Preferences

As we explore the possibilities of culinary innovation, it is crucial to consider the role of consumer preferences. Today's consumers are increasingly health-conscious and environmentally aware, influencing their food choices. The rise of plant-based diets and organic products is a testament to this shift. According to a survey by *Nielsen*, 39% of consumers are willing to pay more for products that are sustainably sourced.

Understanding these preferences is essential for food innovators aiming to create products that resonate with their target audience. Market research and consumer feedback play pivotal roles in shaping product development, ensuring that innovations align with consumer values.

Conclusion

In conclusion, the exploration of possibilities in the future of food is a multifaceted endeavor that requires a deep understanding of theoretical frameworks, identification of existing problems, and a keen awareness of consumer preferences. As culinary innovators like Lee Hernandez continue to push the boundaries of food technology, they pave the way for a more sustainable, equitable, and delicious future. By addressing the challenges of food insecurity and environmental sustainability, the culinary world can transform into a space of creativity and innovation, ultimately enriching the lives of individuals and communities around the globe.

The need for innovation

In today's rapidly evolving world, the food industry faces unprecedented challenges that necessitate innovative solutions. From climate change to population growth, the pressures on food systems are mounting, prompting a re-evaluation of traditional culinary practices and the introduction of cutting-edge technologies.

Addressing Global Challenges

One of the primary drivers of innovation in the food sector is the urgent need to address global challenges. According to the United Nations, the global population is projected to reach approximately 9.7 billion by 2050, which will require a 70% increase in food production to meet the demand [?]. This monumental task is complicated by factors such as:

+ **Climate Change**: Alterations in weather patterns are affecting crop yields and food security, necessitating the development of climate-resilient crops and sustainable farming practices.

+ **Resource Scarcity**: With freshwater resources dwindling and arable land becoming increasingly scarce, innovative techniques such as vertical farming and aquaponics are gaining traction as viable solutions.

+ **Food Waste**: Approximately one-third of all food produced globally is wasted, amounting to about 1.3 billion tons annually [?]. Innovations in food preservation, packaging, and distribution are critical to reducing this waste.

Technological Advancements

The integration of technology into food production and preparation has opened new avenues for innovation. For example, advancements in biotechnology have led to the development of genetically modified organisms (GMOs) that can withstand pests and diseases, thereby increasing crop yields. Furthermore, techniques such as CRISPR gene editing enable precise modifications to DNA, offering the potential for enhanced nutritional profiles and improved food security.

In addition, the rise of artificial intelligence (AI) and machine learning is transforming food supply chains. AI algorithms can analyze vast amounts of data to optimize planting schedules, predict harvest yields, and even personalize dietary recommendations for consumers based on their health data. As noted by [?], the food industry is beginning to embrace these technologies to improve efficiency and sustainability.

Consumer Demand for Sustainability

Today's consumers are increasingly aware of the environmental and ethical implications of their food choices. A survey conducted by [?] found that 66% of global respondents are willing to pay more for sustainable brands. This shift in consumer behavior has prompted food companies to innovate in areas such as:

+ **Plant-Based Alternatives**: The popularity of plant-based diets has led to a surge in the development of meat substitutes, such as those produced by companies like Beyond Meat and Impossible Foods. These products not only cater to dietary preferences but also aim to reduce the environmental impact associated with livestock farming.

+ **Sustainable Packaging**: Innovations in biodegradable and compostable packaging materials are becoming essential as consumers seek to minimize their ecological footprint. Companies are now exploring alternatives to traditional plastics, such as packaging made from seaweed or mushroom mycelium.

The Role of Culinary Innovators

Culinary innovators like Lee Hernandez are at the forefront of this transformation, leveraging their expertise to create solutions that resonate with both consumers and the environment. By embracing food technology and sustainability, these innovators are not just responding to market demands but actively shaping the future of food.

For instance, Hernandez's development of FlavorBurst™ exemplifies how innovation can enhance flavor while also considering dietary restrictions and sustainability. This product not only provides unique taste experiences but also addresses the growing demand for healthier, plant-based options.

Conclusion

The need for innovation in the food industry is driven by a confluence of global challenges, technological advancements, and changing consumer preferences. As the world navigates these complexities, culinary innovators will play a crucial role in redefining food systems, ensuring that future generations have access to nutritious, sustainable, and delicious food. It is through their creativity and commitment to innovation that we can hope to forge a resilient food future.

Meet Lee Hernandez, a culinary prodigy

Lee Hernandez, a name that has become synonymous with culinary innovation, emerged from humble beginnings in a vibrant food-centric family. Born in the heart of New Orleans, a city renowned for its rich culinary heritage, Lee was surrounded by the aromas of spices and the sounds of sizzling pans from an early age. His family, with roots tracing back to generations of cooks and food enthusiasts, instilled in him a profound appreciation for the art and science of cooking.

From the moment he could reach the countertop, Lee was drawn to the kitchen. His first culinary experiment involved mixing flour, water, and a sprinkle of salt to create a dough that, while not quite bread, was a testament to his early curiosity and creativity. This moment marked the inception of a lifelong passion for food that would eventually lead him to redefine the culinary landscape.

A Natural Flair for Flavors

Lee's innate talent for flavor combinations became apparent during family gatherings, where he would often take the lead in preparing dishes. His grandmother's gumbo was a family favorite, but Lee's rendition introduced an unexpected twist by incorporating elements of molecular gastronomy. By utilizing spherification techniques, he created flavorful spheres that burst with essence when bitten, transforming a traditional dish into an avant-garde experience. This innovative approach not only delighted his family but also sparked conversations about the future of food among local chefs.

Recognition from Local Chefs

As his culinary prowess blossomed, Lee caught the attention of local chefs who recognized his potential. At the age of sixteen, he was invited to participate in a regional culinary competition, where he showcased his signature dish: a deconstructed jambalaya featuring smoked chicken, shrimp foam, and a delicate rice gel. The dish not only earned him the title of Young Chef of the Year but also garnered praise for its creativity and technical execution.

This recognition fueled Lee's ambition to explore the intersection of culinary arts and technology. He began to delve into the science behind cooking, studying the chemical reactions that occur during the cooking process. For instance, he learned about the Maillard reaction, which is responsible for the browning and flavor development in cooked meats. Understanding these principles would later become instrumental in his approach to food technology.

The Call of Culinary School

Encouraged by his early successes, Lee decided to pursue formal culinary education. He enrolled at the prestigious Institute of Culinary Arts, where he was exposed to a rigorous curriculum that emphasized both traditional cooking techniques and modern culinary science. Under the guidance of renowned chefs and educators, he honed his skills in various cuisines, mastering everything from classic French techniques to contemporary fusion dishes.

At the Institute, Lee's passion for innovation blossomed further. He began to experiment with new technologies, such as 3D food printing and cryogenic cooking, which allowed him to push the boundaries of what was considered possible in the culinary world. His projects often challenged the status quo, leading to spirited discussions among his peers and professors about the future of food and the role of technology in shaping culinary experiences.

Early Experiments with Food Technology

Lee's early experiments with food technology included creating edible films that could encapsulate flavors, allowing for a unique tasting experience. For example, he developed a film infused with the essence of basil that could be placed on top of a dish, adding a burst of fresh flavor as it melted away. This innovative technique not only showcased his creativity but also highlighted the potential for food technology to enhance traditional culinary practices.

By the time he graduated, Lee had already established himself as a culinary prodigy, with a portfolio of innovative dishes and a deep understanding of food science. His journey was just beginning, as he prepared to embark on a path that would lead him to revolutionize the food industry through technology and creativity.

In conclusion, Lee Hernandez's early years were marked by a blend of tradition and innovation. His upbringing in a food-centric family, coupled with his natural talent and formal education, set the stage for a remarkable career in culinary technology. As we delve deeper into his story, it becomes clear that Lee's journey is not just about personal success; it is about redefining the future of food for generations to come.

Overview of the book

In this book, we embark on a culinary journey through the life and innovations of Lee Hernandez, a visionary in the realm of food technology. The narrative is structured to not only present the remarkable achievements of Hernandez but also to delve into the broader implications of his work on the future of food. We will explore how culinary innovation is essential in addressing the challenges of a rapidly changing world, from food security to sustainability.

The Structure of the Book

The book is organized into several key sections, each designed to highlight different aspects of Hernandez's life and career. The narrative begins with an exploration of the future of food, setting the stage for understanding the critical need for innovation in this sector. We will discuss the global challenges that necessitate a rethinking of how we produce, consume, and think about food.

Thematic Elements

A central theme of this book is the intersection of culinary art and science. We will examine how Hernandez's early experiences in a food-centric family laid the foundation for his culinary talent. The discussion will include the significance of early exposure to cooking and flavor experimentation, which can be likened to the concept of *experiential learning* as proposed by Kolb (1984), where knowledge is gained through the transformation of experience into knowledge.

$$\text{Experiential Learning} = \text{Concrete Experience} + \text{Reflective Observation} + \text{Abstract Conce} \tag{4}$$

This equation illustrates how Hernandez's formative years were not just about cooking but about learning through doing, reflecting on those experiences, and applying them in innovative ways.

Challenges and Triumphs

As we progress through the chapters, we will highlight the challenges Hernandez faced in culinary school and during his apprenticeship at Xperimental Foods Inc. These experiences are not merely anecdotes; they are reflective of the broader struggles faced by many innovators in the food technology space. We will analyze the importance of resilience and adaptability in overcoming obstacles, drawing parallels with the *Growth Mindset* theory posited by Dweck (2006), which emphasizes the belief that abilities can be developed through dedication and hard work.

$$\text{Growth Mindset} = \text{Belief in Development} + \text{Effort} + \text{Learning from Failure} \tag{5}$$

This framework will help us understand how Hernandez's mindset contributed to his success in creating groundbreaking food products like FlavorBurst™.

Culinary Innovations and Sustainability

In the later chapters, we will delve into the revolutionary impact of Hernandez's work on the food industry, particularly in terms of sustainability and reducing food waste. We will explore how his entrepreneurial ventures, such as Culinary Innovations Inc., have not only transformed the culinary landscape but also addressed pressing global issues. For example, we will analyze the role of technology in enhancing food production efficiency, which can be modeled by the equation:

$$\text{Food Production Efficiency} = \frac{\text{Output (nutritional value)}}{\text{Input (resources used)}} \tag{6}$$

This equation highlights the necessity for innovators to maximize output while minimizing resource input, a principle that Hernandez has embraced in his work.

Legacy and Future Outlook

Finally, the book will culminate in a reflection on Hernandez's legacy and the future of food technology. We will discuss how his journey serves as an inspiration for aspiring food innovators, emphasizing the importance of mentorship and community in fostering the next generation of culinary talent. This section will provide insights into the potential future trends in food technology, including the integration of artificial intelligence and biotechnology, and how these innovations may further reshape our food systems.

In summary, this book not only chronicles the life of Lee Hernandez but also serves as a comprehensive exploration of the future of food technology. It aims to inspire readers to think critically about the food they consume and the innovations that drive the industry forward, making it a vital read for anyone interested in the culinary arts, food science, and sustainability.

Setting the stage for the future

The future of food is not merely a canvas of culinary artistry but a complex tapestry woven from the threads of technology, sustainability, and cultural evolution. As we delve into the possibilities that lie ahead, it is essential to understand the multifaceted challenges we face in the food industry today. The global population is projected to reach approximately 9.7 billion by 2050, necessitating a dramatic increase in food production, estimated to be around 70% more than what we produce today [1]. This demand poses significant challenges, including resource scarcity, climate change, and the need for sustainable practices.

One of the primary theories shaping the future of food is the concept of *sustainable food systems*. This theory advocates for a holistic approach to food production that not only meets the nutritional needs of the population but also minimizes environmental impact. For instance, the adoption of regenerative agricultural practices can enhance soil health, increase biodiversity, and sequester carbon, thereby addressing climate change while boosting food security [2].

Moreover, the rise of food technology has opened new avenues for innovation. Techniques such as *vertical farming, hydroponics,* and *aeroponics* are redefining how we grow food. By utilizing controlled environments, these methods can significantly reduce the land and water needed for cultivation. For example, a study by Al-Kodmany (2018) highlights that vertical farms can produce up to 10 times more food per square foot than traditional farms, all while using 90% less water.

In parallel, the integration of biotechnology into food production is paving the way for genetically modified organisms (GMOs) that are more resilient to climate stresses and pests. The application of CRISPR technology, for instance, allows for precise editing of plant genomes, leading to crops that can withstand drought conditions or have enhanced nutritional profiles [4]. However, these advancements are not without controversy, as public perception and regulatory challenges continue to influence the adoption of such technologies.

As we explore these innovations, it is crucial to consider the socio-economic implications. The digital divide remains a significant barrier, particularly in developing countries where access to technology is limited. According to the World Bank, approximately 1.7 billion people lack access to basic financial services, which hinders their ability to invest in or benefit from new food technologies [5]. Addressing these disparities is essential for ensuring that the benefits of food innovation are equitably distributed.

Furthermore, the cultural dimensions of food cannot be overlooked. The future of food must embrace the diversity of culinary traditions while fostering inclusivity. The rise of fusion cuisine exemplifies this trend, as chefs blend flavors and techniques from different cultures to create innovative dishes that resonate with a global audience. This cross-pollination of culinary practices not only enriches the dining experience but also promotes cultural exchange and understanding.

In summary, setting the stage for the future of food requires a multifaceted approach that encompasses sustainability, technological innovation, socio-economic equity, and cultural appreciation. As we embark on this journey,

Lee Hernandez stands at the forefront, embodying the spirit of innovation that will shape the culinary landscape of tomorrow. His pioneering work in food technology serves as a beacon of hope, illustrating how creativity and science can converge to address the pressing challenges of our time.

Bibliography

[1] Food and Agriculture Organization. (2017). *The future of food and agriculture: Trends and challenges.*

[2] Regenerative Agriculture Initiative. (2020). *Regenerative Agriculture: A Global Perspective.*

[3] Al-Kodmany, R. (2018). *The Vertical Farm: A Review of Developments and Impacts.*

[4] CRISPR Research Group. (2021). *Advancements in CRISPR Technology for Food Production.*

[5] World Bank. (2020). *The Global Financial Inclusion Database.*

Early Years: A Taste for Innovation

Birth and upbringing in a food-centric family

Growing up in the kitchen

From an early age, Lee Hernandez's life revolved around the kitchen, a bustling hub of creativity and flavor that shaped his future as a culinary innovator. In a family where food was not merely sustenance but a form of expression, Lee was immersed in a world where the kitchen served as a classroom, a laboratory, and a sanctuary. This environment fostered not only his culinary skills but also a profound understanding of the cultural significance of food.

The Kitchen as a Learning Space

The kitchen can be viewed through the lens of experiential learning theory, particularly Kolb's Experiential Learning Cycle, which emphasizes the importance of concrete experiences, reflective observation, abstract conceptualization, and active experimentation. Lee's early experiences in the kitchen exemplified this cycle:

- **Concrete Experience:** Lee's first memories include standing on a stool, peering over the counter as his grandmother kneaded dough for her famous empanadas. The tactile sensation of flour on his hands and the smell of baking bread created a sensory-rich environment that sparked his curiosity.

- **Reflective Observation:** As he watched family members cook, Lee began to notice the nuances of flavor combinations and cooking techniques. He observed how the same ingredients could yield vastly different results based on the method of preparation, leading him to ponder the science behind cooking.

+ **Abstract Conceptualization:** Lee began to formulate theories about flavor pairing and the importance of technique. Inspired by his grandmother's recipes, he started to document his observations, creating a notebook filled with notes on various dishes and their preparation methods.

+ **Active Experimentation:** Encouraged by his family, Lee began experimenting with his own recipes. He would often modify traditional family dishes, adding his unique twist, which not only delighted his family but also ignited a passion for culinary innovation.

Influence of Family Traditions

Family traditions played a pivotal role in shaping Lee's culinary identity. Each meal was a celebration of heritage, where recipes were passed down through generations, rich with stories and memories. The kitchen became a space of cultural exchange, where Lee learned to appreciate the significance of food in bringing people together.

For instance, during family gatherings, the preparation of traditional dishes like tamales and pozole was a communal effort. Lee learned the importance of collaboration and teamwork, as each family member contributed their skills to create a feast. This experience not only honed his culinary abilities but also instilled a sense of pride in his cultural roots.

The First Experiments with Food

Lee's initial forays into cooking were marked by a mix of enthusiasm and naivety. At the age of eight, he decided to surprise his family by preparing dinner. Armed with a cookbook and a desire to impress, he set out to make spaghetti from scratch. However, the experience was fraught with challenges:

$$\text{Time Taken} = \text{Preparation Time} + \text{Cooking Time} + \text{Cleanup Time} \quad (7)$$

Lee quickly learned that while the preparation time seemed manageable, the cooking and subsequent cleanup took much longer than anticipated. Despite the chaos, including a minor sauce explosion that left the kitchen looking like a tomato war zone, the dish turned out surprisingly well. His family's laughter and praise solidified his love for cooking, teaching him that even mistakes could lead to memorable experiences.

Natural Flair for Flavors

As Lee grew older, his natural flair for flavors became evident. He began to experiment with spices and herbs, understanding their role in enhancing dishes. His family's diverse culinary background provided a rich tapestry of flavors to explore. Lee would often combine elements from different cuisines, creating unique fusion dishes that showcased his creativity.

For example, one of his early signature dishes was a taco-inspired sushi roll, which combined traditional Japanese ingredients with Mexican flavors. This innovative approach not only surprised his family but also sparked discussions about the endless possibilities of culinary creativity.

Recognition from Local Chefs

Lee's burgeoning talent did not go unnoticed. Local chefs, recognizing his potential, began to mentor him. They invited him to shadow them in their kitchens, providing insights into professional cooking techniques and the culinary arts. These experiences were instrumental in shaping his understanding of the industry and the importance of continual learning.

Through these interactions, Lee learned about the significance of presentation and the science of cooking. He was introduced to the concept of umami, the fifth taste, which further fueled his desire to explore the complexities of flavor. He began to appreciate how different cooking methods, such as roasting versus steaming, could dramatically alter the taste and texture of ingredients.

Conclusion

Growing up in the kitchen provided Lee Hernandez with a solid foundation for his culinary journey. The combination of family traditions, hands-on experiences, and mentorship from local chefs cultivated his passion for food and innovation. This early exposure not only shaped his skills but also instilled a deep appreciation for the role of food in culture and community. As he moved forward in his culinary career, the lessons learned in his childhood kitchen would continue to influence his approach to food technology and innovation.

Influences from family traditions

Lee Hernandez's culinary journey was deeply rooted in the rich tapestry of family traditions that surrounded him from a young age. Growing up in a food-centric family, he was immersed in a culture where food was not merely sustenance but a form of expression, connection, and love. This section explores how these familial influences shaped his culinary identity and fostered his innovative spirit.

Culinary Heritage

The culinary heritage of the Hernandez family was a vibrant blend of cultural influences, primarily stemming from their Mexican roots. Traditional dishes such as *tamales*, *pozole*, and *mole* were staples at family gatherings, each prepared with recipes passed down through generations. These recipes were not just instructions; they were narratives filled with stories of family history and cultural significance. For instance, the preparation of *mole* was a communal activity, often involving multiple family members, each contributing their unique touch to the dish. This practice instilled in Lee a profound respect for the art of cooking and the importance of collaboration in the kitchen.

Celebration of Food

Family celebrations were often centered around food, reinforcing the idea that meals were a means of bringing people together. Birthdays, holidays, and even simple Sunday dinners were occasions for the family to gather around the table, sharing not just food but also laughter and stories. This ritual highlighted the role of food as a social glue, fostering bonds and creating lasting memories. Lee learned early on that food could evoke emotions and serve as a conduit for connection, which would later influence his approach to culinary innovation.

Lessons from Elders

Lee's grandmother, a formidable figure in the kitchen, was particularly influential in shaping his culinary philosophy. She often emphasized the importance of using fresh, locally-sourced ingredients, a principle that Lee would carry into his future endeavors. Her insistence on quality over convenience instilled in him a deep appreciation for the origins of food and the impact of sourcing on flavor and sustainability. This lesson became foundational in his later work in food technology, where he sought to create products that honored the integrity of ingredients while pushing the boundaries of flavor.

Culinary Creativity and Experimentation

While family traditions provided a strong foundation, they also encouraged creativity. Lee was often encouraged to experiment with traditional recipes, adding his own flair and modern twists. For example, during family gatherings, he would often introduce new flavors or techniques, such as incorporating molecular gastronomy principles into classic dishes. This blend of tradition and innovation became a hallmark of his culinary style, allowing him to honor his roots while also exploring new frontiers in food.

Theoretical Framework: Cultural Identity in Culinary Arts

The influence of family traditions on culinary practices can be understood through the lens of cultural identity theory. According to *Hall's Theory of Cultural Identity*, cultural identity is not a fixed essence but a constantly evolving construct shaped by historical narratives, social practices, and individual experiences [?]. In Lee's case, his culinary identity was forged through the interplay of familial expectations, cultural heritage, and personal creativity. This dynamic process allowed him to navigate and reinterpret traditional culinary practices, ultimately leading to his innovative contributions to the food industry.

Challenges and Solutions

While family traditions provided a rich foundation, they also presented challenges. Lee often grappled with the tension between honoring traditional recipes and pursuing modern culinary trends. For instance, he faced criticism from family members when he experimented with plant-based versions of beloved meat dishes, such as *carnitas*. This conflict highlighted the broader challenges faced by many chefs who seek to innovate while respecting the cultural significance of traditional foods. Lee's solution was to engage in open dialogue with his family, explaining the rationale behind his innovations and seeking their input. This approach not only helped bridge the gap between tradition and modernity but also reinforced the values of respect and collaboration that were central to his upbringing.

Conclusion

In conclusion, the influences from family traditions played a pivotal role in shaping Lee Hernandez's culinary identity. The rich cultural heritage, the celebration of food as a social activity, the lessons learned from elders, and the encouragement of creativity all contributed to his development as a culinary innovator. By weaving together the threads of tradition and modernity, Lee was able to carve out a unique space in the culinary world, one that honored his roots while embracing the future of food technology.

The first experiments with food

Lee Hernandez's culinary journey began long before he stepped into a formal kitchen; it was rooted in the simple yet profound experiences of his childhood. From a young age, Lee exhibited an insatiable curiosity about food, which manifested in his first experiments in the kitchen. These early forays were not merely about following recipes but about understanding the underlying principles of flavor and texture, laying the groundwork for his future innovations.

Curiosity and Creativity

At the tender age of eight, Lee took his first steps into the world of culinary experimentation. Armed with his grandmother's old recipe book and a set of mismatched kitchen utensils, he began to explore the possibilities of combining ingredients. His first experiment involved a classic dish: a simple tomato sauce. However, instead of following the recipe to the letter, Lee decided to add an unconventional twist—he incorporated a splash of balsamic vinegar and a pinch of cinnamon.

This bold choice was not without its challenges. Initially, the flavors clashed, resulting in a sauce that was more perplexing than palatable. Yet, this experience taught him a crucial lesson about balance in flavor profiles, a principle that would become central to his culinary philosophy. The equation for balance in flavor can be expressed as:

$$\text{Flavor Balance} = \frac{\text{Sweetness} + \text{Acidity} + \text{Bitterness} + \text{Umami}}{\text{Texture}}$$

Where each component plays a vital role in achieving a harmonious dish. Lee learned that while sweetness and acidity can enhance a dish, they must be carefully measured against the overall texture to achieve the desired outcome.

The Science of Cooking

As Lee continued to experiment, he began to delve deeper into the science behind cooking. He discovered that cooking is not just an art but also a science, governed by chemical reactions and physical transformations. For instance, he learned about the Maillard reaction, which occurs when proteins and sugars react under heat, resulting in the browning of food and the development of complex flavors.

This knowledge prompted him to conduct a series of experiments with different cooking methods. One notable experiment involved roasting vegetables at varying temperatures. Lee meticulously recorded the outcomes, noting how the caramelization process altered the taste and texture of carrots and bell peppers. His findings can be summarized as follows:

$$Flavor\ Development = f(Temperature, Time, Moisture\ Content)$$

Where f represents the function of how these variables interact to enhance or diminish flavor. Through trial and error, Lee discovered that roasting at a higher temperature for a shorter duration produced a sweeter, more concentrated flavor, while lower temperatures resulted in a more tender, albeit less flavorful, vegetable.

Inspiration from Nature

Lee's early experiments were also inspired by the natural world around him. He often ventured into his backyard, where he would forage for herbs and edible flowers. This connection to nature not only enriched his culinary repertoire but also instilled a profound respect for seasonal ingredients.

One of his most memorable experiments involved creating a dish using freshly picked wild garlic. He decided to make a pesto, but instead of using traditional pine nuts, he opted for sunflower seeds, which were more accessible. The resulting dish was a vibrant green sauce that burst with flavor, showcasing the power of fresh ingredients. Lee's approach can be encapsulated in the following principle:

$$Freshness = Flavor\ Intensity \times Seasonal\ Relevance$$

This equation highlights the importance of using seasonal ingredients to maximize flavor, a concept that would later influence his innovative approaches in food technology.

Lessons Learned

Through these early experiments, Lee learned invaluable lessons that shaped his culinary identity. The importance of creativity, the role of science in cooking, and the value of fresh, seasonal ingredients became cornerstones of his approach. Each failure served as a stepping stone toward understanding the complexities of flavor and texture, ultimately leading to his later successes.

In conclusion, Lee Hernandez's first experiments with food were not just about creating dishes; they were about exploration, learning, and growing as a culinary innovator. These formative experiences laid the groundwork for his future endeavors in food technology, where he would continue to push the boundaries of what is possible in the culinary world.

Early signs of culinary talent

Natural flair for flavors

Lee Hernandez's journey into the world of culinary innovation began with an innate ability to discern and combine flavors in ways that were both surprising and delightful. This natural flair for flavors is not merely a matter of taste; it encompasses a deep understanding of the science behind flavor profiles, the cultural contexts of food, and the emotional connections that flavors can evoke.

Understanding Flavor Profiles

Flavor is a complex interplay of taste, aroma, and mouthfeel, which can be broken down into several basic tastes: sweet, sour, salty, bitter, and umami. The ability to balance these elements is crucial for any chef. Research in food science has shown that the human palate is incredibly sensitive to these tastes, and even slight variations can significantly alter the overall perception of a dish.

The foundational equation that describes flavor perception can be expressed as:

$$F = T + A + M \tag{8}$$

where F represents the overall flavor perception, T is the taste, A is the aroma, and M is the mouthfeel. This equation illustrates how each component contributes to the overall experience of flavor.

Cultural Influences on Flavor Combinations

Growing up in a food-centric family, Lee was exposed to a myriad of culinary traditions, each with its unique flavor combinations. This exposure allowed him to develop a keen sense of how different cultures utilize ingredients to create harmonious dishes. For instance, the use of umami-rich ingredients like soy sauce in Asian cuisine contrasts with the Mediterranean's reliance on fresh herbs and citrus to achieve brightness in flavor.

Lee's ability to draw from these diverse influences is exemplified in his signature dish, *Fusion Tacos*, which marry traditional Mexican flavors with Asian-inspired ingredients. The dish features a soft corn tortilla filled with marinated pulled pork, pickled vegetables, and a drizzle of sriracha-infused crema. This combination not only showcases Lee's flair for flavors but also reflects a broader trend in contemporary cuisine towards fusion and experimentation.

Emotional Connections to Flavor

Flavor is not just a sensory experience; it also evokes memories and emotions. Lee Hernandez understood early on that food has the power to transport individuals back to specific moments in their lives. This concept is supported by research in psychology, which suggests that flavor and aroma are closely linked to memory. The brain's limbic system, which is responsible for emotions and memories, is activated by the olfactory signals from food.

For example, the smell of freshly baked bread might remind someone of their grandmother's kitchen, creating a sense of nostalgia and comfort. Lee's ability to tap into these emotional connections allows him to create dishes that resonate with people on a personal level. He often incorporates ingredients that have sentimental value to him and his family, such as heirloom tomatoes from his childhood garden or spices that remind him of family gatherings.

Experimentation and Innovation

Lee's natural flair for flavors also manifests in his willingness to experiment with unconventional combinations. This innovative spirit is a hallmark of successful chefs and food technologists. By understanding the fundamental principles of flavor and the science behind ingredient interactions, Lee was able to push the boundaries of traditional cooking.

One notable example of his experimentation is his development of a *Savory Chocolate Mousse*, which combines dark chocolate with a hint of chili and sea salt. This dish challenges the conventional perception of chocolate as a sweet treat, showcasing how flavors can be manipulated to create surprising and delightful experiences.

The underlying chemistry that allows for such innovations can be explained through the concept of *flavor synergy*, where certain ingredients enhance each other's flavors when combined. The equation for flavor synergy can be represented as:

$$S = T_1 + T_2 + (T_1 \cdot T_2) \tag{9}$$

where S is the synergistic flavor, and T_1 and T_2 represent the individual flavors. This equation illustrates how the combination of flavors can produce a more complex and enjoyable taste experience than the sum of their parts.

Conclusion

In conclusion, Lee Hernandez's natural flair for flavors is a blend of scientific understanding, cultural influences, emotional connections, and a spirit of experimentation. His journey exemplifies how a chef can transcend traditional boundaries by embracing innovation and creativity in the kitchen. This innate talent, coupled with a relentless pursuit of culinary excellence, has set the stage for Lee's future contributions to the world of food technology and culinary arts.

Creative recipe inventions

Lee Hernandez's journey into the realm of culinary innovation was marked by his innate ability to blend flavors and textures in ways that left a lasting impression on those fortunate enough to taste his creations. This section delves into the creative process behind his recipe inventions, exploring the theoretical foundations, challenges faced, and notable examples that highlight his genius.

Theoretical Foundations of Recipe Creation

At the heart of recipe invention lies a deep understanding of flavor profiles, which can be analyzed through the lens of food science. The concept of *flavor pairing* suggests that certain ingredients work harmoniously together based on their chemical compounds. For instance, the combination of strawberries and basil is not merely a coincidence; both ingredients share similar aromatic compounds, making them a perfect match in a dish.

The Maillard reaction is another crucial theory that informs culinary creativity. This complex chemical reaction occurs when proteins and sugars are heated, resulting in the browning of food and the development of complex flavors. Understanding this reaction allows chefs like Hernandez to experiment with cooking techniques that enhance the overall taste of their dishes.

Challenges in Recipe Development

Despite the theoretical knowledge, the path to creating a successful recipe is fraught with challenges. One of the primary obstacles is balancing flavors. A dish that is overly salty or sweet can overshadow the intended taste experience. Hernandez often employed the *five basic tastes*—sweet, sour, salty, bitter, and umami—as a framework for developing his recipes.

Another challenge is the textural interplay of ingredients. The mouthfeel of a dish can significantly affect the perception of flavor. For example, combining crispy elements with creamy sauces can create a delightful contrast that enhances the dining experience. Hernandez's ability to manipulate textures was evident in his signature dish, *Crispy Quinoa with Avocado Mousse*, where the crunch of the quinoa perfectly complemented the smoothness of the avocado.

Examples of Creative Recipe Inventions

Hernandez's creative prowess is best illustrated through some of his most notable recipe inventions. One such example is his *Saffron-Infused Risotto with Citrus Foam*. In this dish, he leveraged the aromatic properties of saffron, which is known for its ability to elevate dishes with its unique flavor and vibrant color. By incorporating a citrus foam, Hernandez introduced a refreshing element that brightened the richness of the risotto, showcasing his skill in balancing flavors.

Another standout creation is the *Spicy Chocolate Ganache Tart*. This dessert exemplifies Hernandez's mastery of flavor pairing, as he combined the richness of dark chocolate with the heat of chili peppers. The result was a complex dessert that tantalized the palate with its unexpected heat, challenging traditional notions of dessert flavors.

The Role of Feedback in Recipe Development

An essential aspect of Hernandez's creative process was the incorporation of feedback. After developing a new recipe, he would often host tasting sessions with friends and fellow chefs. This collaborative approach allowed him to refine his dishes based on constructive criticism. For instance, during one tasting, a colleague suggested that the *Saffron-Infused Risotto* needed more acidity to balance the richness. Taking this feedback into account, Hernandez experimented with different citrus elements until he found the perfect balance.

Conclusion

In summary, Lee Hernandez's creative recipe inventions are a testament to his understanding of culinary science, his ability to overcome challenges, and his willingness to adapt based on feedback. By merging theoretical knowledge with practical experimentation, he has carved a niche for himself in the culinary world, inspiring others to push the boundaries of flavor and creativity. The recipes he developed not only tantalized taste buds but also paved the way for future innovations in the food industry.

Recognition from local chefs

As Lee Hernandez began to refine his culinary skills, it was not long before his talent caught the attention of local chefs and food enthusiasts. Recognition from established figures in the culinary world can serve as a crucial stepping stone for emerging talents, providing validation and opportunities that can significantly influence a young chef's career trajectory.

The Impact of Recognition

The acknowledgment from local chefs can be understood through the lens of social capital theory, which posits that social networks and relationships can provide individuals with access to resources, information, and opportunities. In the culinary world, endorsements from respected chefs can open doors to apprenticeships, competitions, and collaborations, which are vital for professional growth.

$$\text{Social Capital} = \text{Network Strength} \times \text{Resource Access} \qquad (10)$$

In Lee's case, the recognition he received from local chefs not only validated his skills but also expanded his network, allowing him to gain insights into the industry and learn from the best.

Local Culinary Competitions

During his formative years, Lee participated in several local culinary competitions, where he showcased his innovative dishes. These events served as a platform for him to demonstrate his creativity and technical prowess. One notable competition was the annual *Taste of the Future*, where young chefs presented their signature dishes to a panel of esteemed local chefs.

Lee's entry, a deconstructed version of a classic dish, not only impressed the judges but also sparked conversations about his approach to food. The judges, including renowned chef Maria Gonzalez, praised his ability to blend traditional techniques with modern interpretations. This recognition led to an invitation to intern at Maria's restaurant, a pivotal moment in Lee's culinary journey.

Mentorship and Guidance

The recognition from local chefs also translated into mentorship opportunities. Chefs often take young talents under their wings, providing guidance and sharing invaluable industry insights. For instance, after receiving accolades at a local food festival, Lee was mentored by Chef Tom Rivers, a celebrated figure known for his innovative fusion cuisine.

Chef Rivers emphasized the importance of understanding the science behind cooking, encouraging Lee to explore the molecular gastronomy that would later become a cornerstone of his culinary style. This mentorship not only honed Lee's skills but also instilled in him a deep appreciation for the culinary arts.

Building a Reputation

As Lee continued to innovate and impress, his reputation grew within the local culinary scene. Recognition from chefs often leads to word-of-mouth endorsements, which can significantly enhance a chef's visibility. Local chefs began to feature Lee's dishes in their restaurants, providing him with a platform to reach a broader audience.

One such instance was when Chef Amanda Lee, a local celebrity chef, invited Lee to collaborate on a special tasting menu for her restaurant's anniversary. This collaboration allowed Lee to showcase his unique flavor combinations and garnered positive reviews from food critics, further solidifying his standing in the culinary community.

Challenges and Overcoming Skepticism

However, the path to recognition is not without its challenges. Many young chefs face skepticism, particularly when introducing unconventional ideas. Lee encountered this when he proposed a unique dish that combined unexpected ingredients. Some local chefs were hesitant to embrace his innovative approach, fearing it might alienate traditional diners.

To overcome this skepticism, Lee conducted a series of informal tastings, inviting local chefs to sample his creations. By gathering feedback and making adjustments based on their critiques, he was able to refine his dishes and demonstrate that innovation could coexist with tradition. This proactive approach not only won over skeptics but also earned him respect as a thoughtful and adaptable chef.

Conclusion

In summary, the recognition from local chefs played a pivotal role in Lee Hernandez's early culinary journey. It provided him with mentorship, opportunities for collaboration, and a platform to showcase his talents. As he navigated the challenges of skepticism and competition, the support and validation from established chefs helped him to cultivate his unique culinary voice, setting the stage for his future innovations in food technology. The relationships he built during this formative period were instrumental in shaping his career and establishing his reputation as a culinary prodigy.

Culinary School: Cultivating Skills

Enrollment at the prestigious Institute of Culinary Arts

Exciting curriculum and renowned professors

The Institute of Culinary Arts is renowned for its rigorous and innovative curriculum, designed to equip aspiring chefs and food technologists with the skills necessary to thrive in an ever-evolving culinary landscape. Lee Hernandez's experience at this prestigious institution was marked by a blend of traditional culinary techniques and cutting-edge food science, providing a holistic approach to gastronomy.

Curriculum Overview

The curriculum at the Institute of Culinary Arts is structured into several key components:

- **Fundamental Cooking Techniques:** Students begin their journey with foundational courses in knife skills, cooking methods, and flavor profiling. Mastery of these techniques is crucial, as they form the basis of all culinary creations. For instance, understanding the Maillard reaction, represented by the equation:

$$\text{Amino Acids} + \text{Reducing Sugars} \rightarrow \text{Brown Pigments (Melanoidins)} + \text{Flavor Compo}$$

is essential for achieving the perfect sear on a steak.

- **Food Science:** The integration of food science into the curriculum allows students to explore the chemical and physical properties of food. Courses cover topics such as emulsification, fermentation, and the role of pH in cooking. For example, students learn about the importance of pH in the process of pickling, where the equation:

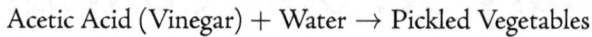

$$\text{Acetic Acid (Vinegar)} + \text{Water} \rightarrow \text{Pickled Vegetables}$$

illustrates how acidity preserves food and enhances flavor.

- **Molecular Gastronomy:** A highlight of the curriculum is the molecular gastronomy module, where students experiment with techniques that transform the dining experience. This includes spherification, foaming, and gelification. An example of spherification is represented by the equation:

$$\text{Sodium Alginate} + \text{Calcium Chloride} \rightarrow \text{Gelled Spheres}$$

which allows for the creation of caviar-like pearls from fruit juices.

- **Sustainable Practices:** In response to global food challenges, the curriculum emphasizes sustainability. Students learn to source ingredients responsibly and reduce waste through innovative practices. For instance, the concept of farm-to-table is explored, highlighting the equation:

$$\text{Local Ingredients} + \text{Seasonal Cooking} \rightarrow \text{Sustainable Cuisine}$$

which encourages chefs to minimize their carbon footprint.

- **Culinary Business Management:** Recognizing the importance of entrepreneurship in the culinary field, the program includes courses on business management, marketing, and financial planning. Students are taught to create business plans that incorporate culinary innovation, using case studies of successful food startups as examples.

Renowned Professors

The faculty at the Institute of Culinary Arts is composed of industry veterans and thought leaders who bring a wealth of experience and knowledge to the classroom. Their diverse backgrounds enrich the educational experience and inspire students to push the boundaries of culinary arts.

- **Chef Maria Rodriguez:** A pioneer in sustainable cooking, Chef Maria emphasizes the importance of local sourcing and seasonal ingredients. Her classes often involve field trips to local farms, where students learn the significance of understanding the origin of their food. Chef Maria's philosophy is encapsulated in her mantra:

  > "Cooking is not just about ingredients; it's about the stories they tell."

- **Dr. Thomas Chen:** An expert in food science, Dr. Chen teaches the molecular gastronomy module. His research on flavor compounds has been published in numerous scientific journals. He encourages students to think critically about the science behind cooking, often challenging them with thought-provoking questions such as:

  > "How can we manipulate texture to enhance the dining experience?"

- **Chef Alex Kim:** Known for his innovative fusion cuisine, Chef Kim teaches students to embrace creativity and experimentation. His classes often involve brainstorming sessions where students collaborate to create unique dishes that blend various culinary traditions. He believes that:

  > "The best dishes are born from curiosity and a willingness to take risks."

- **Professor Linda Patel:** A business strategist, Professor Patel guides students through the entrepreneurial aspects of the culinary world. Her practical approach includes real-world simulations where students pitch their culinary startup ideas to a panel of investors. She emphasizes the importance of a strong business model, stating:

  > "A great dish is only as good as the plan behind it."

Conclusion

The exciting curriculum and the expertise of renowned professors at the Institute of Culinary Arts provided Lee Hernandez with a solid foundation in both culinary skills and food technology. The combination of hands-on experience, scientific understanding, and entrepreneurial insight prepared him to become a trailblazer in the culinary world. The lessons learned during this transformative period would shape his innovative spirit and set the stage for his future endeavors in food technology.

Challenges and triumphs in the kitchen

Culinary school is often portrayed as a glamorous journey filled with the tantalizing aroma of freshly baked bread and the vibrant colors of seasonal produce. However, for Lee Hernandez, the reality was a rigorous battleground where every dish was a test of skill, creativity, and resilience. The challenges he faced in the kitchen were as diverse as the ingredients he worked with, and each triumph was hard-earned, shaping him into the innovative chef he would become.

One of the primary challenges Lee encountered was the intense pressure of culinary school. The environment was competitive, with students vying for the attention of renowned chefs and striving to outshine one another. This competition often led to high-stress situations, where the fear of failure loomed large. As Lee quickly learned, the kitchen was not just about cooking; it was a high-stakes arena where every mistake could be magnified.

$$\text{Stress Level} = \frac{\text{Pressure from Peers} + \text{Expectations from Instructors}}{\text{Support from Classmates}} \quad (11)$$

In this equation, the balance between pressure and support became crucial. Lee found that fostering relationships with his classmates provided a buffer against the overwhelming stress. They formed study groups, shared tips, and supported one another during practical exams. This camaraderie not only alleviated some of the pressure but also enhanced their collective culinary skills.

Another significant challenge was mastering the technical skills required for various cooking techniques. From knife skills to sauce-making, each technique demanded precision and practice. Lee often struggled with the classic French technique of *sous-vide*, where food is cooked slowly in a water bath at precisely controlled temperatures. The science behind it intrigued him, yet achieving the perfect texture and flavor proved elusive.

To overcome this hurdle, Lee dedicated countless hours to practice. He meticulously recorded his experiments, adjusting cooking times and temperatures based on the results. This iterative process is well encapsulated in the following formula:

$$\text{Flavor Profile} = f(\text{Cooking Time}, \text{Temperature}, \text{Ingredients}) \quad (12)$$

Here, f represents the function that determines how the interplay of time, temperature, and ingredients can yield a desired flavor profile. After numerous attempts, Lee finally mastered sous-vide, creating tender, flavorful dishes that impressed both his instructors and peers.

Triumphs in the kitchen were often accompanied by moments of serendipity. One such instance occurred during a class focused on creating sauces. Lee, while experimenting with a basic *béchamel*, accidentally added a hint of smoked paprika instead of the intended nutmeg. The unexpected twist resulted in a uniquely flavorful sauce that elevated the dish beyond its traditional roots. This experience highlighted the importance of creativity and spontaneity in cooking, teaching Lee that sometimes, the best innovations come from unplanned moments.

$$\text{Innovation} = \text{Creativity} + \text{Experimentation} \tag{13}$$

In this equation, Lee recognized that embracing creativity and experimentation could lead to groundbreaking culinary innovations. This philosophy would later influence his approach to food technology, encouraging him to push the boundaries of traditional cooking.

As Lee progressed through culinary school, he also faced the challenge of time management. Balancing rigorous coursework, practical exams, and personal life required exceptional organizational skills. He developed a system that prioritized tasks based on deadlines and complexity, ensuring that he allocated sufficient time for both study and practice.

$$\text{Time Allocation} = \frac{\text{Total Hours}}{\text{Tasks}} \tag{14}$$

This formula allowed him to maximize his productivity, ensuring that he could dedicate time to each culinary discipline without compromising his overall performance.

Ultimately, the challenges Lee faced in the kitchen were integral to his growth as a chef. Each obstacle taught him valuable lessons about resilience, creativity, and the importance of collaboration. The triumphs, whether big or small, fueled his passion for culinary arts and laid the groundwork for his future innovations in food technology.

In conclusion, the kitchen was not merely a place to learn how to cook; it was a crucible of challenges and triumphs that shaped Lee Hernandez into a culinary innovator. The skills he honed, the relationships he built, and the lessons he learned would serve him well as he embarked on his journey into the world of food technology, where the stakes were even higher, and the potential for innovation was limitless.

Forming lifelong friendships

Culinary school is not just a place for honing one's skills in the kitchen; it is a vibrant environment where bonds are forged, experiences are shared, and lifelong friendships are formed. For Lee Hernandez, his time at the prestigious Institute of Culinary Arts was pivotal not only for his culinary development but also for the relationships that would support him throughout his career.

The Importance of Camaraderie

The kitchen can be an intense and high-pressure environment. Students often work long hours, facing the rigors of culinary techniques and the demands of their instructors. In such a setting, camaraderie becomes essential. Research in social psychology suggests that shared experiences, particularly those involving stress, can significantly strengthen interpersonal bonds. According to the *Social Penetration Theory* proposed by Altman and Taylor, relationships develop in stages, moving from superficial interactions to deeper, more intimate connections as individuals share personal experiences and vulnerabilities.

During his time at culinary school, Lee found that the shared challenges of mastering complex recipes and techniques fostered a unique bond among his peers. They became each other's support system, celebrating successes and providing encouragement during failures. This sense of community not only enhanced their culinary education but also cultivated friendships that would extend beyond the walls of the school.

Collaboration and Teamwork

One of the most significant aspects of culinary education is the emphasis on teamwork. Students often work in groups to prepare meals, manage kitchens, and execute events. This collaborative environment teaches valuable lessons about trust, communication, and compromise—skills that are vital in any professional setting. Lee's experience in these collaborative projects was instrumental in forming strong friendships.

For example, during a particularly challenging module on international cuisines, Lee and his classmates were tasked with creating a multi-course dinner featuring dishes from various cultures. The project required not only culinary skills but also effective collaboration and planning. Lee's role as a team leader allowed him to connect with his peers on a deeper level, as they navigated the complexities of menu planning, ingredient sourcing, and time management together. This shared endeavor not only resulted in a successful dinner but also solidified friendships that would last a lifetime.

Networking Beyond the Classroom

The relationships formed in culinary school often extend into the professional realm. As students graduate and begin their careers, the network of friends and colleagues becomes a valuable resource. Lee Hernandez exemplified this phenomenon when he and his classmates began to support each other's entrepreneurial ventures after graduation.

For instance, one of Lee's classmates, Sarah, launched a successful food truck business specializing in gourmet tacos. Lee, recognizing the potential for collaboration, offered to develop a unique line of sauces for her menu. This partnership not only boosted Sarah's business but also allowed Lee to experiment with new flavors and techniques, further enhancing his culinary portfolio. Such collaborations illustrate the importance of maintaining connections made during culinary school, as they can lead to mutually beneficial opportunities in the future.

Lifelong Bonds Through Shared Passion

The shared passion for food and innovation is a powerful catalyst for forming lasting friendships. Lee and his classmates often spent hours discussing culinary trends, experimenting with new recipes, and exploring the science behind food. These discussions not only enriched their knowledge but also deepened their connections.

A study published in the *Journal of Applied Psychology* found that individuals who share a common interest are more likely to develop strong, lasting relationships. Lee's passion for food technology resonated with several of his classmates, leading to late-night brainstorming sessions about future culinary innovations. These moments of creativity and collaboration fostered a sense of belonging and camaraderie that would endure long after graduation.

Challenges and Growth

While forming friendships in culinary school is often a rewarding experience, it is not without its challenges. Conflicts can arise due to differing personalities, competition, and stress. Lee encountered several instances where disagreements occurred over culinary techniques or project responsibilities. However, these challenges also served as opportunities for growth.

Conflict resolution is a critical skill in both culinary arts and personal relationships. Lee learned to navigate these situations by practicing active listening and empathy, allowing him to understand his peers' perspectives. This approach not only helped to resolve conflicts but also strengthened the bonds between him and his classmates, as they learned to appreciate each other's strengths and weaknesses.

Conclusion

In conclusion, the friendships formed during culinary school played a vital role in shaping Lee Hernandez's career and personal life. The shared experiences, collaborative projects, and mutual passion for food created a strong network of support that would last well beyond their time at the Institute of Culinary Arts. As Lee navigated the challenges of the culinary world, he drew strength from these lifelong friendships, demonstrating that the bonds formed in the kitchen can be just as important as the skills learned there. The lessons learned about teamwork, communication, and empathy would serve him well as he ventured into the ever-evolving landscape of food technology, reinforcing the idea that culinary education is as much about building relationships as it is about mastering the art of cooking.

Discovering a passion for food technology

Introduction to molecular gastronomy

Molecular gastronomy is a sub-discipline of food science that explores the physical and chemical transformations of ingredients that occur in cooking. It is both a culinary art and a scientific inquiry, merging the worlds of gastronomy and molecular science to create innovative cooking techniques and flavors. This section will delve into the principles of molecular gastronomy, its significance in the culinary world, and the challenges it presents to chefs and food technologists alike.

Theoretical Foundations

At its core, molecular gastronomy is grounded in the understanding of the molecular structure of food. The discipline applies principles from chemistry and physics to analyze how ingredients interact at the molecular level during cooking. This includes understanding how heat, pressure, and various cooking techniques affect the texture, flavor, and appearance of food.

One of the key theories in molecular gastronomy is the concept of *emulsification*. Emulsification is the process of mixing two immiscible liquids, such as oil and water, to create a stable mixture. The stability of an emulsion is often enhanced by the use of *emulsifiers*, which are compounds that reduce the surface tension between the two liquids. For example, lecithin, found in egg yolks, is a common emulsifier used in making mayonnaise.

Mathematically, the stability of an emulsion can be described using the *Young-Laplace equation*:

$$\Delta P = \gamma \left(\frac{1}{R_1} + \frac{1}{R_2} \right) \tag{15}$$

where ΔP is the pressure difference across the interface, γ is the surface tension, and R_1 and R_2 are the principal radii of curvature of the droplet. This equation illustrates how the curvature of droplets in an emulsion affects their stability.

Techniques and Applications

Molecular gastronomy encompasses a variety of techniques that enhance the culinary experience. Some notable techniques include:

- **Spherification:** This technique involves creating small spheres filled with liquid, which burst in the mouth to release flavor. It typically uses sodium alginate and calcium chloride to create a gel-like membrane around the liquid. The reaction can be represented as follows:

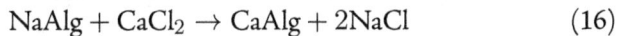

$$NaAlg + CaCl_2 \rightarrow CaAlg + 2NaCl \tag{16}$$

  where sodium alginate reacts with calcium chloride to form calcium alginate, which creates the gel structure.

- **Foaming:** This technique involves incorporating air or gas into a liquid to create a foam. Common foaming agents include lecithin and gelatin. The stability of foams can be analyzed using the *Foam Stability Equation*, which considers factors like surface tension and viscosity.

- **Sous-vide:** This method involves vacuum-sealing food in a bag and cooking it to a very precise temperature in a water bath. This technique allows for enhanced flavor retention and texture control. The temperature control can be mathematically modeled using the *Fourier's Law of Heat Conduction*:

$$q = -k\frac{dT}{dx} \qquad (17)$$

where q is the heat transfer rate, k is the thermal conductivity, dT is the temperature difference, and dx is the distance over which the temperature change occurs.

Challenges in Molecular Gastronomy

Despite its innovative potential, molecular gastronomy presents several challenges. One significant issue is the accessibility of specialized equipment and ingredients, which can be cost-prohibitive for many chefs. Additionally, the scientific nature of molecular gastronomy can be intimidating, leading some chefs to shy away from its techniques.

Moreover, there is an ongoing debate regarding the authenticity of molecular gastronomy as a culinary art form. Critics argue that it detracts from traditional cooking methods and the appreciation of natural flavors. This tension between tradition and innovation is a recurring theme in the culinary world.

Examples of Molecular Gastronomy in Practice

Several renowned chefs have embraced molecular gastronomy, pushing the boundaries of culinary creativity. One notable example is Ferran Adrià, the former head chef of elBulli, who is credited with popularizing molecular gastronomy. His signature dish, *Spherical Olive*, exemplifies the spherification technique, delivering an unexpected burst of flavor that transforms the dining experience.

Another example is Heston Blumenthal, known for his experimental approach to cooking. His dish, *Sound of the Sea*, incorporates edible sand and a soundscape of ocean waves to create a multisensory experience that engages both taste and hearing.

Conclusion

In conclusion, molecular gastronomy represents a fascinating intersection of science and culinary art. By understanding the molecular interactions of ingredients, chefs can innovate and create new textures, flavors, and experiences for diners. While challenges remain, the potential for culinary innovation through molecular gastronomy is vast, and it continues to inspire a new generation of chefs and food technologists to explore the endless possibilities of food.

Exploring the science of food

The intersection of food and science is a dynamic field that has garnered significant attention in recent years. Understanding the science behind food not only enhances culinary techniques but also enables innovators like Lee Hernandez to develop groundbreaking products that redefine our culinary experiences. This section explores the fundamental scientific principles that underpin food technology, highlighting key theories, prevalent challenges, and illustrative examples.

The Role of Chemistry in Cooking

At the heart of food science lies chemistry, which explains how ingredients interact during cooking processes. The Maillard reaction, for instance, is a complex chemical reaction between amino acids and reducing sugars that gives browned food its distinctive flavor. This reaction typically occurs at temperatures above 140-165°C (285-329°F) and is responsible for the rich flavors of roasted meats, baked bread, and caramelized vegetables.

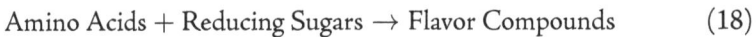

$$\text{Amino Acids} + \text{Reducing Sugars} \rightarrow \text{Flavor Compounds} \tag{18}$$

Understanding this reaction allows chefs to manipulate cooking times and temperatures to achieve desired flavors and textures. For example, a chef might choose to sear a steak at high heat to initiate the Maillard reaction, creating a flavorful crust while keeping the interior juicy.

Physics of Cooking Techniques

Physics also plays a crucial role in food preparation. Techniques such as sous-vide cooking, which involves vacuum-sealing food in a bag and cooking it in a water bath at precise temperatures, rely on principles of thermodynamics. This method ensures that food is cooked evenly and retains moisture, resulting in tender and flavorful dishes.

The formula for heat transfer can be expressed as:

$$Q = mc\Delta T \tag{19}$$

Where:

- Q is the heat energy absorbed or released,

- m is the mass of the substance,

+ c is the specific heat capacity, and

+ ΔT is the change in temperature.

By understanding heat transfer, chefs can optimize cooking methods to achieve the perfect texture and flavor profile.

Biology and Food Safety

Food science is also deeply intertwined with biology, particularly in the realm of food safety. Microbiology, the study of microorganisms, is essential for understanding foodborne pathogens and spoilage organisms. The control of bacteria such as Salmonella and E. coli is critical in preventing foodborne illnesses.

The growth of bacteria can be modeled by the equation:

$$N(t) = N_0 e^{rt} \tag{20}$$

Where:

+ $N(t)$ is the number of bacteria at time t,

+ N_0 is the initial number of bacteria,

+ r is the growth rate, and

+ t is time.

This equation illustrates how quickly bacteria can multiply under favorable conditions, emphasizing the importance of proper food handling and storage practices.

The Impact of Food Structure

The structure of food at the molecular level significantly influences its sensory properties, including taste, texture, and aroma. Emulsions, foams, and gels are examples of food structures that can be manipulated to create innovative culinary experiences.

For instance, the creation of a stable emulsion, such as mayonnaise, involves the dispersion of fat droplets in an aqueous phase. The stability of emulsions can be explained by the Gibbs adsorption isotherm, which describes the relationship between surface tension and the concentration of surfactants:

$$\Gamma = -\frac{1}{RT}\left(\frac{d\gamma}{d\ln C}\right) \tag{21}$$

Where:

+ Γ is the surface excess concentration of the surfactant,

+ γ is the surface tension,

+ R is the universal gas constant, and

+ T is the absolute temperature.

By understanding these principles, chefs can create stable emulsions that enhance the flavor and mouthfeel of their dishes.

Food Technology Innovations

Innovations in food technology are often rooted in scientific exploration. Techniques such as molecular gastronomy leverage scientific principles to create novel dining experiences. For example, the use of liquid nitrogen to create instant ice cream demonstrates the application of cryogenics in food preparation, resulting in a creamy texture that is difficult to achieve through traditional methods.

Moreover, the development of plant-based proteins and alternative ingredients is a response to the growing demand for sustainable food sources. Understanding the molecular composition of these ingredients enables food technologists to replicate the taste and texture of animal products, paving the way for innovations in the culinary world.

Challenges in Food Science

Despite the advancements in food science, several challenges remain. One pressing issue is food waste, which poses significant environmental and economic concerns. Innovative solutions, such as utilizing food by-products in new formulations, are being explored to mitigate this problem.

Additionally, the quest for healthier food options necessitates a deeper understanding of nutritional science. Balancing flavor with health benefits requires a nuanced approach to ingredient selection and processing techniques.

Conclusion

Exploring the science of food is a journey that reveals the intricate relationships between ingredients, cooking techniques, and sensory experiences. As Lee Hernandez continues to innovate in the culinary realm, his understanding of the scientific principles behind food will undoubtedly fuel his creativity and drive for excellence. By embracing the science of food, future innovators can push the boundaries of culinary arts, creating not only delicious but also sustainable and health-conscious food experiences.

Pioneering new techniques and methods

In the realm of food technology, Lee Hernandez became a trailblazer by developing innovative techniques that transformed the culinary landscape. His approach combined scientific principles with artistic expression, leading to the creation of new methods that enhanced flavors, textures, and overall dining experiences.

Molecular Gastronomy: The Science of Flavor

One of the most significant contributions from Hernandez was his deep dive into molecular gastronomy, a field that merges food science with culinary arts. This discipline involves understanding the physical and chemical transformations that occur during cooking. By applying techniques such as spherification, gelification, and emulsification, Hernandez was able to create dishes that surprised and delighted diners.

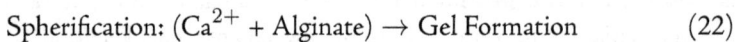

$$\text{Spherification: } (Ca^{2+} + \text{Alginate}) \rightarrow \text{Gel Formation} \qquad (22)$$

Spherification, for instance, involves the use of sodium alginate and calcium chloride to create spheres that burst in the mouth, releasing intense flavors. This technique allows chefs to encapsulate liquids, creating an explosion of taste that challenges traditional perceptions of texture in food.

Emulsification Techniques

Emulsification is another area where Hernandez made strides. Traditional emulsification techniques involve the mixing of two immiscible liquids, such as oil and water, to create stable emulsions like mayonnaise. However, Lee introduced high-energy emulsification methods using ultrasonic waves to achieve finer emulsions with improved stability and texture.

Emulsion Stability: (Viscosity) + (Surface Tension) $\rightarrow$ Stable Emulsion (23)

By manipulating the viscosity of the liquids and reducing surface tension, Hernandez's methods allowed for the creation of lighter, airier emulsions that could elevate dishes to new heights.

Cryogenic Techniques

Cryogenic cooking techniques also became a hallmark of Hernandez's culinary style. By utilizing liquid nitrogen, he was able to instantly freeze ingredients, creating unique textures and preserving the integrity of flavors. This method not only allowed for the creation of innovative desserts but also facilitated the development of new flavor profiles.

For example, by flash-freezing fruits, Hernandez could create a powder that retained the original taste while providing a completely different mouthfeel. This technique also opened avenues for creating ice creams with intense flavors without the need for traditional churning methods.

Fermentation and Flavor Enhancement

Hernandez was also a pioneer in the use of fermentation as a means of enhancing flavors. By harnessing the power of beneficial bacteria and yeasts, he created complex flavor profiles that could not be achieved through conventional cooking methods. Fermented ingredients like miso, kimchi, and kombucha became staples in his culinary repertoire.

The theory behind fermentation is rooted in biochemistry, where microorganisms break down sugars into acids, gases, or alcohol. This process not only enhances the flavor but also increases the nutritional value of the food.

$$\text{Fermentation: } C_6H_{12}O_6 \rightarrow 2C_2H_5OH + 2CO_2 \quad (24)$$

In this equation, glucose is converted into ethanol and carbon dioxide, showcasing how fermentation can transform simple ingredients into culinary masterpieces.

D Food Printing: A New Frontier

Hernandez's innovative spirit also led him to explore 3D food printing technology. This cutting-edge method allows chefs to create intricate designs and shapes that are not feasible with traditional cooking methods. By using edible pastes, Hernandez could print complex structures, leading to visually stunning presentations.

The process involves a computer-controlled printer that deposits layers of food material, allowing for precise control over texture and flavor combinations. The implications of this technology extend beyond aesthetics; it enables customization for dietary restrictions and personal preferences.

Challenges and Solutions

While pioneering these techniques, Hernandez faced several challenges. One of the primary issues was the skepticism from traditional chefs and food critics who viewed these methods as gimmicks rather than genuine culinary advancements. To combat this, Hernandez focused on education and collaboration, hosting workshops and demonstrations to showcase the practicality and artistry of his techniques.

Another challenge was the accessibility of high-tech equipment. Hernandez worked tirelessly to make these innovations available to aspiring chefs by advocating for educational programs and partnerships with culinary schools. By fostering an environment of learning and experimentation, he aimed to democratize food technology.

Conclusion

Through his relentless pursuit of innovation, Lee Hernandez not only transformed the culinary landscape but also inspired a new generation of chefs to embrace the science of food. His pioneering techniques and methods have paved the way for a future where culinary arts and technology coexist harmoniously, creating extraordinary dining experiences that challenge our perceptions of flavor and texture. As Hernandez continues to push the boundaries, the culinary world eagerly anticipates the next wave of innovations that will emerge from his kitchen.

Journey Into Food Technology: Breaking Boundaries

Apprenticeship at Xperimental Foods Inc

Immersion in the world of food technology

The culinary landscape has undergone a seismic shift with the advent of food technology, a field that marries the art of cooking with the precision of science. As Lee Hernandez embarked on his apprenticeship at Xperimental Foods Inc., he found himself at the forefront of this exciting intersection, where innovation flourished and traditional culinary boundaries were expanded.

Food technology encompasses a wide range of disciplines, including food chemistry, microbiology, and engineering. Each plays a critical role in the development of new food products and processes. For instance, understanding the molecular structure of ingredients enables chefs and technologists to manipulate flavors and textures in ways previously thought impossible. This is particularly evident in the realm of molecular gastronomy, a sub-discipline that Lee would soon embrace wholeheartedly.

$$\text{Flavor} = f(\text{Chemical Composition}, \text{Temperature}, \text{Texture}) \qquad (25)$$

In this equation, flavor is a function of several variables, including the chemical composition of the ingredients, the temperature at which they are prepared, and their texture. Lee learned to appreciate how each of these elements could be adjusted to create a desired sensory experience. For example, by altering the temperature during the cooking process, one could enhance or diminish certain flavor compounds, thereby transforming a dish's overall profile.

During his early days at Xperimental Foods, Lee was introduced to the concept of **food preservation** through technology. This included techniques such as freeze-drying, high-pressure processing, and the use of natural preservatives. Each method aims to extend the shelf life of food while maintaining its nutritional value and sensory appeal. Lee observed firsthand how these technologies could revolutionize the way food is stored and consumed, particularly in an era where sustainability and waste reduction are paramount.

$$\text{Shelf Life} = \frac{\text{Quality}}{\text{Rate of Deterioration}} \tag{26}$$

In this equation, shelf life is directly proportional to the quality of the food and inversely proportional to the rate of deterioration. Lee's exposure to innovative preservation techniques sparked his interest in developing products that not only tasted great but also contributed to reducing food waste—a significant global issue.

Moreover, Lee delved into the science of **emulsification**, a process that combines two immiscible liquids, such as oil and water, into a stable mixture. This is crucial in creating sauces, dressings, and other culinary staples. He learned about the role of emulsifiers, such as lecithin, in stabilizing these mixtures and how the manipulation of particle size could affect texture and mouthfeel.

$$\text{Viscosity} = \eta \cdot \frac{dv}{dy} \tag{27}$$

Here, viscosity (η) is a measure of a fluid's resistance to flow, and it is influenced by the rate of shear ($\frac{dv}{dy}$). Understanding these principles allowed Lee to experiment with different emulsification techniques, leading to the creation of unique sauces that elevated traditional dishes to new heights.

As Lee immersed himself in this world of food technology, he also faced challenges. One significant problem was the skepticism surrounding the intersection of science and culinary arts. Many traditional chefs viewed technology as a threat to the authenticity of cooking. Lee had to navigate these waters carefully, often engaging in discussions with seasoned professionals to advocate for the potential benefits of food technology.

A pivotal moment in his apprenticeship came when Lee collaborated with a team of food scientists to develop a new ingredient designed to enhance flavor without the need for excessive salt or sugar. This initiative aligned with the growing demand for healthier food options, and it was met with both excitement and resistance from various sectors of the food industry.

Through hands-on experience, Lee learned to conduct sensory evaluations, a crucial aspect of food technology that assesses how consumers perceive food products. This involved organizing taste tests, gathering feedback, and making iterative improvements based on consumer preferences. The process was not without its hurdles; there were instances where the initial product failed to meet expectations, prompting Lee to return to the drawing board and rethink his approach.

In conclusion, Lee Hernandez's immersion in the world of food technology at Xperimental Foods Inc. was a transformative experience. It equipped him with the knowledge and skills necessary to innovate within the culinary field while addressing contemporary challenges such as sustainability and health. This foundation would later empower him to create groundbreaking products that not only tantalized the taste buds but also made a significant impact on the food industry as a whole.

Collaborating with renowned scientists

During his apprenticeship at Xperimental Foods Inc., Lee Hernandez found himself surrounded by some of the most brilliant minds in the field of food technology. The collaboration with renowned scientists not only enhanced his culinary skills but also expanded his understanding of the scientific principles underlying food innovation. This section delves into the dynamics of these collaborations, the theoretical frameworks they employed, the challenges they faced, and the groundbreaking results they achieved.

Interdisciplinary Approach

Lee quickly learned that food technology is inherently interdisciplinary, merging aspects of chemistry, biology, and engineering. This approach is crucial for innovating new food products and improving existing ones. For instance, the collaboration with food chemist Dr. Evelyn Hartman focused on the molecular composition of flavors. Utilizing principles from *gas chromatography-mass spectrometry (GC-MS)*, they analyzed the volatile compounds responsible for flavor profiles in various ingredients. The equation governing the separation of compounds in GC can be represented as:

$$R_f = \frac{d}{L} \tag{28}$$

where R_f is the retention factor, d is the distance traveled by the substance, and L is the distance traveled by the solvent front. This analytical technique allowed Lee to understand how different compounds interacted and how to manipulate them to create new flavor experiences.

Challenges in Collaboration

Despite the excitement of working with experts, Lee encountered significant challenges. One of the primary issues was the communication barrier between culinary arts and scientific research. Many scientists approached food from a purely analytical perspective, often overlooking the sensory experience that chefs prioritize. To bridge this gap, Lee initiated regular brainstorming sessions where both chefs and scientists could share their insights. This collaborative model facilitated a deeper understanding of the practical implications of scientific research.

For example, during one such session, they discussed the phenomenon of *umami*, the fifth taste, which had been largely underexplored in the culinary world. Dr. Hartman explained the biochemical pathways that lead to umami flavor development, which is primarily attributed to compounds such as glutamate and certain ribonucleotides. This discussion led to the formulation of a new food product that enhanced umami flavor without relying on artificial additives, thereby addressing both health concerns and flavor enhancement.

Innovative Techniques and Applications

One of the most significant outcomes of these collaborations was the development of a novel technique known as *spherification*, which Lee learned from physicist Dr. Marco Chen. Spherification is a process that involves creating spheres of liquid that burst with flavor when bitten into. The fundamental principle behind this technique is the use of sodium alginate and calcium chloride to form a gel-like membrane around a liquid core.

The reaction can be summarized by the following equation:

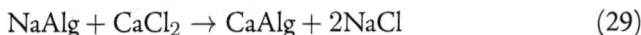

$$NaAlg + CaCl_2 \rightarrow CaAlg + 2NaCl \tag{29}$$

where sodium alginate (NaAlg) reacts with calcium chloride ($CaCl_2$) to form calcium alginate (CaAlg), a gel-like substance that encapsulates the liquid. This technique not only added a visual appeal to dishes but also transformed the dining experience by introducing unexpected bursts of flavor.

Real-World Applications

The practical applications of these collaborations extended beyond the laboratory. Lee and his team tested their innovations in real-world settings, such as local restaurants and food festivals. For instance, they introduced their spherified tomato essence as a garnish for gourmet dishes, which received rave reviews from both chefs and diners. This feedback loop was essential for refining their products and ensuring they met consumer expectations.

Moreover, Lee's team worked with nutritionists to develop products that catered to specific dietary needs, such as gluten-free or low-sodium options. By applying scientific principles to culinary practices, they were able to create healthier alternatives without sacrificing flavor. This was particularly important in addressing the growing demand for health-conscious food choices in the market.

Conclusion

Collaborating with renowned scientists was a transformative experience for Lee Hernandez, shaping his approach to culinary innovation. The interdisciplinary nature of food technology allowed him to push the boundaries of traditional cooking, leading to groundbreaking products that not only delighted the palate but also aligned with modern health trends. Through these collaborations, Lee learned that the fusion of science and culinary art is not just beneficial; it is essential for the future of food. As he continued his journey, the knowledge and skills gained from these experiences would serve as a cornerstone for his future endeavors in the food technology industry.

Pushing the boundaries of culinary innovation

In the rapidly evolving world of food technology, pushing the boundaries of culinary innovation requires a unique blend of creativity, scientific understanding, and practical application. This section delves into the various methodologies and philosophies that Lee Hernandez adopted during his apprenticeship at Xperimental Foods Inc., showcasing how he transformed traditional culinary practices into groundbreaking innovations.

Theoretical Frameworks of Culinary Innovation

At the core of culinary innovation lies the intersection of gastronomy and science. One of the primary theories that Hernandez employed was the concept of *Molecular Gastronomy*, which focuses on the physical and chemical transformations of ingredients that occur during cooking. This theory emphasizes the importance of understanding the science behind cooking processes, allowing chefs to manipulate textures and flavors in unprecedented ways.

$$\text{Flavor} = f(\text{Temperature, pH, Time, Ingredient Composition}) \qquad (30)$$

This equation illustrates the multifactorial nature of flavor development, suggesting that by adjusting these variables, chefs can create entirely new taste experiences. For instance, Hernandez experimented with the Maillard reaction, a chemical reaction between amino acids and reducing sugars that gives browned foods their distinctive flavor. By controlling temperature and time, he was able to enhance the depth of flavor in his dishes, thereby creating a signature style that set him apart in the culinary world.

Challenges in Culinary Innovation

Despite the exciting possibilities that culinary innovation presents, it is not without its challenges. One significant obstacle is the skepticism often encountered from traditionalists within the culinary community. Many chefs view the incorporation of scientific principles into cooking as a departure from the artistry of the craft. Hernandez faced this skepticism head-on, using it as motivation to demonstrate the potential of food technology.

Another challenge is the balance between innovation and palatability. While pushing the boundaries of what is possible, it is crucial to ensure that the end product remains enjoyable and accessible to consumers. Hernandez tackled this challenge by conducting extensive taste tests and gathering feedback from both culinary peers and potential customers. This iterative process allowed him to refine his creations, ensuring that they were not only innovative but also aligned with consumer preferences.

Practical Applications of Innovation

During his time at Xperimental Foods Inc., Hernandez was involved in several groundbreaking projects that exemplified the push for culinary innovation. One notable example was the development of a new line of flavor-enhancing powders, which utilized advanced techniques such as freeze-drying and spherification.

Case Study: FlavorBurst™

The flagship product of Hernandez's innovative efforts was the FlavorBurst™ line, a series of concentrated flavor powders designed to amplify the taste of everyday dishes. The process of creating these powders involved several stages:

1. **Ingredient Selection:** Hernandez and his team selected high-quality ingredients known for their robust flavors, such as heirloom tomatoes and wild mushrooms.

2. **Flavor Extraction:** Using techniques like vacuum distillation, they extracted essential oils and volatile compounds from the ingredients, preserving their aromatic properties while intensifying their flavors.

3. **Powder Production:** The extracted flavors were then transformed into powders through a process of freeze-drying, which removed moisture without compromising the integrity of the flavors.

4. **Testing and Refinement:** The team conducted multiple rounds of testing, adjusting the compositions and ratios to achieve a balanced flavor profile that could be easily incorporated into various dishes.

The success of FlavorBurst™ not only showcased the potential of food technology but also highlighted how innovation could be seamlessly integrated into traditional cooking practices.

Conclusion: A New Era of Culinary Innovation

Lee Hernandez's journey at Xperimental Foods Inc. exemplifies the spirit of pushing culinary boundaries through innovation. By embracing scientific principles, overcoming skepticism, and focusing on practical applications, he laid the groundwork for a new era in the culinary world. His work not only transformed the way flavors are perceived but also inspired a generation of chefs to explore the endless possibilities that food technology offers.

As we look towards the future, it is clear that the fusion of culinary arts and science will continue to drive innovation, challenging chefs to rethink what is possible in the kitchen. Hernandez's contributions serve as a testament to the power of creativity and experimentation in shaping the future of food.

Creating a revolutionary food product

The conception of FlavorBurst™

The journey to create FlavorBurst™ began with a simple yet profound question: how can we enhance the sensory experience of food? Lee Hernandez, driven by his passion for culinary innovation and food technology, sought to develop a product that would revolutionize the way flavors are experienced. The concept of FlavorBurst™ was born out of a synthesis of culinary artistry and scientific exploration, aiming to unlock new taste sensations that could elevate dishes to unprecedented heights.

Understanding Flavor Dynamics

To comprehend the intricacies of FlavorBurst™, it is essential to understand the science behind flavor dynamics. Flavor is a complex interplay of taste, aroma, and mouthfeel, with the primary tastes being sweet, sour, salty, bitter, and umami. The interaction of these tastes with various compounds in food can create a multitude of flavor profiles. According to the *Flavor Wheel*, developed by the flavor industry, the perception of flavor can be represented as follows:

$$F = T + A + M \tag{31}$$

where F represents the overall flavor, T is the taste, A is the aroma, and M is the mouthfeel. This equation illustrates that flavor is not merely a product of taste alone but a combination of several sensory inputs.

Innovative Techniques in Flavor Enhancement

Lee recognized that traditional methods of flavor enhancement were limited in their ability to evoke new sensory experiences. He turned to molecular gastronomy, which utilizes scientific principles to manipulate food at the molecular level. By employing techniques such as spherification, emulsification, and flavor encapsulation, Hernandez aimed to create FlavorBurst™—a product that could deliver intense bursts of flavor in a controlled manner.

One of the key innovations in the development of FlavorBurst™ was the use of *flavor microencapsulation*. This technique involves enclosing flavor compounds within a protective coating, allowing them to be released at specific moments during consumption. The process can be mathematically represented by the following equation, which describes the release kinetics of flavor compounds:

$$R(t) = R_0 \cdot e^{-kt} \tag{32}$$

where $R(t)$ is the amount of flavor released at time t, R_0 is the initial amount of flavor, and k is the rate constant that determines the release speed. By adjusting the parameters of this equation, Hernandez was able to fine-tune the flavor release to create a more dynamic eating experience.

Challenges in Development

The journey to develop FlavorBurst™ was not without its challenges. One of the primary obstacles was overcoming skepticism within the culinary community. Many chefs were resistant to the idea of using technology to enhance food, viewing it as a departure from traditional cooking methods. To address this, Lee conducted a series of blind taste tests, showcasing the enhanced flavors of dishes prepared with FlavorBurst™. The results were overwhelmingly positive, demonstrating that technology could indeed elevate culinary experiences rather than detract from them.

Another significant challenge involved ensuring the stability and safety of the product. Flavor compounds are often volatile and can degrade over time. Hernandez collaborated with food scientists to conduct stability studies, which included varying temperature and pH conditions to determine the optimal storage conditions for FlavorBurst™. The findings led to the development of a proprietary formulation that ensured both flavor integrity and safety, adhering to industry standards.

Successful Launch and Reception

After years of research and development, FlavorBurst™ was officially launched at the annual Food Tech Expo. The product was presented as a versatile flavor enhancer, suitable for both professional chefs and home cooks. The initial reception was phenomenal, with culinary influencers and chefs praising its ability to transform ordinary dishes into extraordinary culinary experiences.

For example, a simple dish of roasted vegetables could be elevated with a few drops of FlavorBurst™ designed to mimic the taste of smoked paprika, providing a rich, smoky flavor without the need for additional cooking time. Such versatility made FlavorBurst™ a staple in modern kitchens, bridging the gap between traditional cooking and innovative food technology.

Conclusion

The conception of FlavorBurst™ marked a significant milestone in Lee Hernandez's journey as a culinary innovator. By merging culinary art with scientific principles, he created a product that not only enhanced flavors but also challenged perceptions of food technology. FlavorBurst™ stands as a testament to the potential of innovation in the culinary world, inspiring a new generation of chefs to explore the boundaries of flavor and creativity.

Unlocking new taste sensations

The culinary landscape is continuously evolving, and the quest to unlock new taste sensations is at the forefront of this transformation. Lee Hernandez, through his innovative work with FlavorBurst™, harnesses the principles of food science and technology to create unprecedented flavor experiences. This section delves into the theoretical underpinnings of taste perception, the challenges faced in flavor innovation, and the groundbreaking examples that illustrate Lee's contributions to the culinary world.

The Science of Taste Perception

Taste is a complex sensory experience that involves the interaction of various components, including taste buds, olfactory receptors, and the brain's interpretation of signals. The primary tastes recognized by the human palate are sweet, sour, salty, bitter, and umami. Recent research has suggested the existence of additional taste modalities, such as fat and kokumi, expanding the landscape of flavor perception.

The interaction of these tastes can be described using the following equation, which models the perception of overall flavor intensity F:

$$F = \sum_{i=1}^{n} w_i \cdot T_i \tag{33}$$

where F is the overall flavor intensity, T_i represents the intensity of each individual taste, and w_i are the corresponding weights reflecting the contribution of each taste to the overall perception.

Challenges in Flavor Innovation

Creating new taste sensations is not without its challenges. One of the primary hurdles is the inherent variability in human taste perception. Factors such as genetics, culture, and personal experiences can significantly influence how flavors are perceived. For instance, a compound that is perceived as sweet by one individual may be interpreted as overly bitter by another. This variability poses a significant challenge for food innovators like Lee, who aim to create universally appealing flavors.

Another challenge lies in the formulation of FlavorBurst™. The product must achieve a delicate balance between flavor intensity and mouthfeel. This balance can be represented by the following equation, which integrates both flavor intensity F and mouthfeel M:

$$S = \frac{F}{M} \tag{34}$$

where S represents the overall sensory satisfaction. A high S value indicates a successful product that delivers both strong flavors and an enjoyable mouthfeel.

Groundbreaking Examples of Flavor Innovation

Lee's work with FlavorBurst™ has resulted in several groundbreaking products that exemplify the unlocking of new taste sensations. One notable example is the development of a flavor-enhancing gel that utilizes molecular gastronomy techniques. This gel is designed to release flavor compounds at controlled rates, allowing consumers to experience a layered flavor profile as they consume the dish.

For instance, consider a dish that incorporates Lee's flavor-enhancing gel with a traditional tomato sauce. The gel could be engineered to release bursts of umami and sweetness at specific intervals during consumption, creating a dynamic taste experience. This innovative approach not only enhances the overall flavor but also engages the consumer's palate in a novel way.

Another example is the use of plant-based ingredients to create flavors that mimic traditional animal-based products. By employing techniques such as fermentation and enzymatic reactions, Lee has developed a plant-based cheese that offers a rich, creamy flavor profile reminiscent of aged dairy cheeses. This innovation not only caters to dietary preferences but also expands the sensory repertoire available to consumers.

Conclusion

Unlocking new taste sensations is a multifaceted endeavor that combines the science of taste perception with creative culinary techniques. Lee Hernandez's work with FlavorBurst™ exemplifies the potential of food technology to transform the culinary landscape. By overcoming the challenges inherent in flavor innovation and leveraging scientific principles, Lee continues to push the boundaries of what is possible in the realm of taste. As we look to the future, the possibilities for new flavor experiences are boundless, promising an exciting journey for both chefs and consumers alike.

Overcoming skepticism in the industry

In the world of culinary innovation, skepticism often looms large, particularly when introducing groundbreaking concepts like FlavorBurst™. This skepticism can stem from various sources, including traditional chefs who hold steadfast to classic culinary principles, consumers wary of new technologies, and even investors who question the viability of novel food products. To navigate this landscape, Lee

Hernandez employed a multifaceted approach that combined education, transparency, and strategic partnerships.

Understanding the Roots of Skepticism

Skepticism in the food industry can be attributed to several factors:

+ **Tradition vs. Innovation:** Many chefs and culinary professionals are deeply rooted in traditional cooking methods and recipes. The introduction of technology into food preparation can be seen as a threat to the authenticity of culinary arts. For instance, molecular gastronomy, which utilizes scientific techniques to create new textures and flavors, often faces criticism from purists who argue that it detracts from the essence of cooking.

+ **Consumer Concerns:** Consumers are increasingly aware of the ingredients in their food and the processes used to create it. The fear of artificial additives or synthetic processes can lead to resistance against innovative products. FlavorBurst™, which utilizes advanced flavor encapsulation techniques, had to overcome the initial hesitation of consumers who equated technology with unnaturalness.

+ **Economic Viability:** Investors often approach new food technologies with caution. The food industry is notoriously challenging, with high failure rates for new products. As such, investors require substantial evidence of market demand and profitability before committing resources.

Strategies to Overcome Skepticism

To counteract this skepticism, Lee Hernandez implemented several strategies:

1. **Education and Outreach:** Hernandez recognized the importance of educating both culinary professionals and consumers about the science behind FlavorBurst™. He organized workshops and tastings that showcased the product's capabilities, allowing chefs to experience firsthand the versatility and potential of the technology. By demystifying the process and emphasizing the culinary artistry involved, he was able to win over many skeptics.

2. **Transparency in Ingredients:** To address consumer concerns, Hernandez prioritized transparency in his product formulations. FlavorBurst™ utilized natural ingredients and avoided artificial additives. This commitment to quality helped

build trust with consumers, as they could see that the innovation did not compromise their health or the integrity of their food.

3. Collaborations with Renowned Chefs: Partnering with well-respected chefs in the industry provided Hernandez with credibility. By collaborating with culinary icons who endorsed FlavorBurst™, Hernandez was able to leverage their reputations to gain acceptance within the culinary community. For example, when Chef Maria Torres, a Michelin-starred chef, incorporated FlavorBurst™ into her menu, it sparked interest and curiosity among her peers.

4. Pilot Programs and Feedback Loops: Hernandez initiated pilot programs in restaurants to gather real-time feedback from chefs and diners. By allowing chefs to experiment with FlavorBurst™ in their kitchens, he created a platform for open dialogue and constructive criticism. This iterative process helped refine the product while also demonstrating its practical applications in a professional setting.

Case Studies of Success

Two notable examples illustrate how Hernandez effectively overcame skepticism:

Case Study 1: The Culinary Institute Showcase During a showcase at the Culinary Institute of America, Hernandez presented a dish featuring FlavorBurst™. The dish, a deconstructed fruit tart, utilized the technology to enhance flavors without adding extra sugar. Critics initially approached the presentation with skepticism, but as they tasted the dish, their perceptions shifted. The unique flavor profile and innovative presentation garnered praise, leading to increased interest in FlavorBurst™.

Case Study 2: The Farmers' Market Initiative Hernandez launched an initiative at local farmers' markets where he provided samples of dishes made with FlavorBurst™ to consumers. The immediate positive feedback from consumers who appreciated the enhanced flavors helped dispel doubts about the technology. Furthermore, Hernandez engaged with local farmers to source ingredients, reinforcing the message of sustainability and community support.

Conclusion

Overcoming skepticism in the food industry requires a strategic approach grounded in education, transparency, and collaboration. By actively engaging with both culinary professionals and consumers, Lee Hernandez was able to transform skepticism into acceptance, paving the way for FlavorBurst™ to revolutionize the culinary landscape.   His journey illustrates that innovation, when approached thoughtfully, can find its place even in the most traditional of industries.

Entrepreneurial Ventures: Building a Food Empire

Launching his own food tech startup

Culinary Innovations Inc. is born

In the heart of a bustling urban landscape, where culinary dreams interweave with technology, Lee Hernandez embarked on an audacious journey to establish his own food tech startup, Culinary Innovations Inc. This venture was not merely a business but a manifestation of his passion for revolutionizing the food industry through innovative technology. The inception of Culinary Innovations Inc. marked a pivotal moment in Lee's career, as he sought to blend his culinary expertise with cutting-edge food science.

The Vision

Lee's vision for Culinary Innovations Inc. was rooted in the belief that food should not only nourish the body but also tantalize the senses and promote sustainability. He envisioned a company that would harness the power of technology to create products that were not only delicious but also environmentally friendly. This vision was guided by the principles of sustainable gastronomy, which emphasizes the importance of sourcing ingredients responsibly and minimizing waste throughout the food production process.

Initial Challenges

The journey to establish Culinary Innovations Inc. was fraught with challenges. Securing funding was one of the most significant hurdles. Lee needed to convince investors that his innovative ideas could translate into a viable business model. He faced skepticism from potential backers who were accustomed to traditional food businesses. To overcome this, Lee developed a comprehensive business plan that outlined his vision, market analysis, and projected financials.

$$\text{Projected Revenue} = \text{Market Size} \times \text{Market Share} \qquad (35)$$

Where: - **Projected Revenue** is the expected income from sales. - **Market Size** refers to the total potential market for food tech innovations. - **Market Share** is the percentage of the market that Culinary Innovations Inc. aims to capture.

Lee's meticulous research demonstrated the increasing demand for innovative food products, particularly those that catered to health-conscious consumers and those with dietary restrictions. His projections indicated a potential market size of $5 billion, with an attainable market share of 2%, leading to a projected revenue of $100 million within the first five years.

Assembling the Team

With a solid business plan in hand, Lee set out to assemble a team of culinary experts and food scientists who shared his vision. He sought individuals who were not only skilled in their respective fields but also passionate about pushing the boundaries of culinary innovation. This diverse team included chefs with experience in molecular gastronomy, food technologists specializing in flavor enhancement, and sustainability experts who could guide the company's eco-friendly initiatives.

The collaborative spirit within Culinary Innovations Inc. was palpable, as team members engaged in brainstorming sessions to develop new product concepts. One of the first projects was the development of a plant-based flavor enhancer that could mimic the umami taste found in traditional animal-based ingredients. This project aimed to cater to the growing vegan and vegetarian market while addressing concerns about sustainability.

Securing Investments and Funding

To turn his vision into reality, Lee organized a series of pitch meetings with potential investors. He utilized a combination of compelling storytelling and data-driven presentations to showcase the potential of Culinary Innovations Inc. During one particularly pivotal meeting, Lee presented a prototype of the plant-based flavor enhancer, demonstrating its versatility and taste profile through a live cooking demonstration.

The response was overwhelmingly positive, leading to several investment offers. Ultimately, Lee secured $2 million in seed funding, which allowed him to set up a state-of-the-art kitchen laboratory and hire additional staff. This funding was critical in transforming Culinary Innovations Inc. from a conceptual idea into a functioning entity.

Launching the Brand

With the team in place and funding secured, Culinary Innovations Inc. officially launched its brand. The company's mission statement—"Innovating Flavor, Inspiring Sustainability"—resonated with consumers and industry professionals alike. Lee and his team focused on creating a product line that emphasized bold flavors, innovative techniques, and sustainable sourcing.

The first product to hit the market was the aforementioned plant-based flavor enhancer, marketed under the name **UmamiBoost**™. This product quickly gained traction, appealing to chefs and home cooks looking to elevate their dishes without compromising on ethical values. The launch was accompanied by a robust marketing campaign that included social media promotions, cooking demonstrations, and partnerships with food influencers.

Conclusion

The birth of Culinary Innovations Inc. represented not just the establishment of a business, but the realization of Lee Hernandez's dream to transform the culinary landscape through innovation. By combining culinary artistry with scientific advancements, Lee set the stage for a new era in food technology, one that prioritized flavor, sustainability, and health. The journey had just begun, but the foundation was laid for a food empire that would leave a lasting impact on the industry and inspire future generations of food innovators.

Assembling a team of culinary experts

In the dynamic landscape of food technology, the formation of a skilled and diverse team is paramount to the success of any culinary venture. Lee Hernandez understood that his vision for Culinary Innovations Inc. could only be realized through the collaborative efforts of experts who brought unique perspectives and skill sets to the table. This section delves into the strategies and considerations that guided Lee in assembling his team of culinary experts.

Identifying Key Roles

The first step in assembling a team was to identify the essential roles that would support the diverse needs of the startup. Lee recognized that a multidisciplinary approach was necessary to tackle the complexities of food technology. The following roles were deemed critical:

- **Food Scientists:** Experts in the chemical and biological properties of food, food scientists play a crucial role in product development. They analyze ingredients, conduct experiments, and ensure that innovations are both safe and effective.

- **Culinary Chefs:** Skilled chefs bring practical kitchen experience and creativity to the team. Their expertise in flavor pairing, presentation, and cooking techniques is invaluable for product development and culinary innovation.

- **Nutritionists:** With a growing focus on health and wellness, nutritionists ensure that products meet dietary guidelines and address consumer health concerns. They provide insights on ingredient selection and nutritional content.

- **Marketing Specialists:** To effectively communicate the brand's vision and products, marketing specialists are essential. They develop strategies to reach target audiences and create compelling narratives around innovations.

- **Supply Chain Managers:** Efficient logistics and sourcing are vital for any food business. Supply chain managers ensure that ingredients are sourced sustainably and that products reach consumers in optimal condition.

Recruitment Strategies

With a clear understanding of the roles needed, Lee implemented several recruitment strategies to attract top talent:

1. **Networking and Industry Events:** Lee attended culinary expos, food technology conferences, and industry networking events to meet potential candidates. This face-to-face interaction allowed him to gauge passion and expertise in a more personal setting.

2. **Collaborations with Culinary Schools:** Establishing partnerships with renowned culinary institutions enabled Lee to tap into a pool of emerging talent. Internships and mentorship programs were created to foster relationships with students and recent graduates.

3. **Online Platforms and Job Boards:** Utilizing professional networking sites such as LinkedIn and specialized job boards for the food industry helped Lee reach a wider audience. Clear job descriptions emphasized the innovative nature of Culinary Innovations Inc., attracting like-minded individuals.

Fostering a Collaborative Environment

Once the team was assembled, Lee focused on fostering a collaborative environment that encouraged creativity and innovation. He implemented several practices to ensure effective teamwork:

+ **Open Communication:** Lee established an open-door policy, encouraging team members to share ideas and feedback freely. Regular brainstorming sessions were held to inspire creativity and problem-solving.

+ **Cross-Disciplinary Projects:** To promote collaboration among different specialties, Lee initiated cross-disciplinary projects where food scientists, chefs, and nutritionists worked together to develop new products. This not only enhanced creativity but also fostered mutual respect among team members.

+ **Continuous Learning:** Recognizing that the food technology landscape is ever-evolving, Lee encouraged team members to pursue continuous education. Workshops, online courses, and industry certifications were supported, ensuring that the team remained at the forefront of innovation.

Challenges in Team Assembly

Despite Lee's strategic approach, several challenges arose during the team assembly process:

+ **Diverse Perspectives:** While diversity can enhance creativity, it can also lead to conflicts if not managed effectively. Lee had to navigate differing opinions and approaches, ensuring that discussions remained constructive and focused on the company's goals.

+ **Balancing Experience and Fresh Talent:** Lee faced the challenge of balancing experienced professionals with fresh talent. While seasoned experts brought valuable insights, younger team members often introduced innovative ideas and perspectives. Striking this balance was crucial for the team's dynamic.

+ **Resource Constraints:** As a startup, Culinary Innovations Inc. faced budget constraints that limited recruitment options. Lee had to be resourceful in attracting talent, often relying on equity options and a compelling vision to entice potential team members.

Successful Outcomes

The efforts put into assembling a strong team yielded significant outcomes for Culinary Innovations Inc. The collaborative environment fostered innovation, leading to the successful development of the FlavorBurst™ product line. The team's diverse expertise allowed for a comprehensive approach to product development, addressing not only taste but also nutritional value and marketability.

Moreover, the successful launch of Culinary Innovations Inc. positioned the company as a leader in the food technology sector, attracting attention from investors and consumers alike. The team's collective efforts demonstrated the power of collaboration in driving culinary innovation.

In conclusion, Lee Hernandez's approach to assembling a team of culinary experts was pivotal to the success of Culinary Innovations Inc. By identifying key roles, employing strategic recruitment methods, fostering collaboration, and overcoming challenges, Lee created a dynamic team capable of pushing the boundaries of food technology. This foundation of expertise and creativity would ultimately allow Culinary Innovations Inc. to thrive in the competitive food industry.

Securing investments and funding

In the competitive landscape of food technology, securing investments and funding is a critical step for any aspiring entrepreneur, including Lee Hernandez. This section explores the strategies, challenges, and successes associated with obtaining the necessary financial backing to launch and expand Culinary Innovations Inc.

Understanding Funding Sources

To navigate the funding landscape, Lee needed to understand the various sources of investment available to startups. These sources generally fall into several categories:

- **Bootstrapping:** This involves using personal savings or revenue generated from early sales to fund the business. While this method maintains full control over the company, it can limit growth potential if funds are insufficient.

- **Angel Investors:** Wealthy individuals who provide capital in exchange for equity. Angel investors often bring valuable industry experience and networks, which can be beneficial for a startup.

- **Venture Capital:** Firms that invest in high-growth potential startups in exchange for equity. Venture capitalists typically seek a significant return on investment, which can pressure entrepreneurs to scale quickly.

- **Crowdfunding:** Platforms like Kickstarter and Indiegogo allow entrepreneurs to raise small amounts of money from a large number of people. This method not only provides funds but also validates the business idea through consumer interest.

- **Grants and Competitions:** Many organizations offer grants or host competitions for innovative food tech solutions. Winning these can provide both funding and exposure.

Crafting a Compelling Pitch

Once Lee identified potential funding sources, the next step was to craft a compelling pitch. A successful pitch typically includes the following components:

- **Problem Statement:** Clearly articulate the problem Culinary Innovations Inc. aims to solve. For instance, Lee could highlight the increasing demand for sustainable food solutions in a world facing climate change.

- **Unique Value Proposition:** What sets FlavorBurst™ apart from existing products? Lee needed to emphasize the innovative aspects of his food technology, such as its ability to enhance flavors without artificial additives.

- **Market Analysis:** Present data on market size, trends, and target demographics. Lee could use statistical models to project future growth, such as:

$$\text{Market Growth Rate} = \frac{\text{Market Size}_{\text{future}} - \text{Market Size}_{\text{present}}}{\text{Market Size}_{\text{present}}} \times 100\%$$

$$(36)$$

where Market Size$_{future}$ is the projected value of the food tech market in five years, and Market Size$_{present}$ is the current value.

+ **Business Model:** Outline how Culinary Innovations Inc. plans to generate revenue, including pricing strategies, distribution channels, and customer acquisition plans.

+ **Financial Projections:** Provide forecasts for revenue, expenses, and profitability over the next three to five years. This could include a break-even analysis:

$$\text{Break-even Point (BEP)} = \frac{\text{Fixed Costs}}{\text{Price per Unit} - \text{Variable Cost per Unit}} \quad (37)$$

where Fixed Costs include overhead expenses, Price per Unit is the selling price of FlavorBurst™, and Variable Cost per Unit includes the costs of ingredients and production.

Building Relationships with Investors

Securing funding is not just about the pitch; it also involves building relationships with potential investors. Lee focused on networking within the food tech community, attending industry conferences, and seeking mentorship from established entrepreneurs. These connections often lead to introductions to investors who are interested in innovative food solutions.

Challenges in Securing Funding

Despite Lee's best efforts, he faced several challenges in securing investments:

+ **Skepticism:** Many investors were initially skeptical about the viability of FlavorBurst™ and the food tech industry as a whole. Lee had to provide substantial evidence and testimonials to counter these doubts.

+ **Competition:** The food technology sector is highly competitive, with numerous startups vying for attention and funding. Lee had to differentiate his company and demonstrate a clear competitive advantage.

+ **Economic Climate:** External economic factors, such as recessions or shifts in consumer spending, can impact investor willingness to fund new ventures. Lee had to adapt his pitch to address these concerns and show resilience.

Success Stories and Lessons Learned

Ultimately, Lee's persistence paid off. After several rounds of pitching and refining his business model, he secured funding from a combination of angel investors and a successful crowdfunding campaign. This not only provided the necessary capital to launch Culinary Innovations Inc. but also validated his concept in the eyes of the market.

> "Securing investments is a journey, not a destination. Each 'no' brings you closer to a 'yes'—you just have to keep refining your approach and believing in your vision." — Lee Hernandez

In conclusion, securing investments and funding is a multifaceted process that requires a deep understanding of the funding landscape, a compelling pitch, strong networking, and resilience in the face of challenges. Lee Hernandez's journey exemplifies how determination and innovation can lead to success in the competitive world of food technology.

Expanding the product line

Diversity in textures and flavors

The culinary landscape has evolved dramatically over the years, with an increasing emphasis on the diversity of textures and flavors in food. This section delves into how Lee Hernandez's innovations have embraced this diversity, creating a tapestry of sensory experiences that cater to a wide array of palates and dietary needs.

Understanding Texture and Flavor

Texture and flavor are fundamental components of culinary art. Texture refers to the physical feel of food, often described in terms such as crunchy, creamy, chewy, or velvety. Flavor, on the other hand, encompasses the complex interplay of taste and aroma, involving five basic tastes: sweet, sour, salty, bitter, and umami. The combination of these elements can evoke emotions, memories, and cultural connections, making them essential in food innovation.

The Science Behind Texture

The perception of texture is influenced by several factors, including the size and shape of food particles, moisture content, and temperature. For instance, the

Maillard reaction, a chemical reaction between amino acids and reducing sugars that gives browned foods their distinctive flavor, also contributes to texture. The equation representing the Maillard reaction can be simplified as:

$$\text{Amino acids} + \text{Reducing sugars} \xrightarrow{\text{Heat}} \text{Flavor compounds} + \text{Brown pigments} \quad (38)$$

This reaction is crucial in developing the crispy crust of a roasted chicken or the golden-brown exterior of a loaf of bread.

Innovative Textural Combinations

Lee Hernandez's approach to food technology emphasizes the importance of innovative textural combinations. By utilizing techniques such as spherification, he has transformed traditional ingredients into unexpected forms. For example, his use of alginate allows the creation of caviar-like spheres that burst with flavor when bitten, providing a unique textural experience. This technique not only enhances the dish visually but also adds an element of surprise, engaging the diner's senses.

Flavor Pairing: A New Paradigm

In addition to texture, flavor pairing has become a focal point in Hernandez's culinary innovations. The concept of flavor pairing is grounded in the idea that certain ingredients share common flavor compounds, leading to harmonious combinations. This principle can be illustrated through the use of the Flavor Network, which maps out the relationships between ingredients based on their chemical compositions.

For example, the pairing of strawberries and balsamic vinegar is not only a classic combination but is also supported by the presence of similar flavor compounds such as esters and phenols. Hernandez's culinary innovations often explore these relationships, resulting in dishes that surprise and delight.

Catering to Diverse Dietary Needs

A significant aspect of Hernandez's work is his commitment to inclusivity in food design. By focusing on diversity in textures and flavors, he addresses the needs of various dietary restrictions, including gluten-free, vegan, and low-sodium diets.

For instance, the development of a gluten-free bread that mimics the texture of traditional sourdough is a testament to this commitment. By incorporating alternative flours such as almond or chickpea flour, Hernandez achieves a satisfying chew while maintaining the beloved sourdough flavor profile. The use of hydrocolloids like xanthan gum further enhances the texture, providing structure and moisture retention.

Culinary Examples of Diversity

Hernandez's product line exemplifies the diversity of textures and flavors. One standout example is his line of plant-based snacks, which feature a combination of crunchy, crispy, and creamy textures. The use of air-fried chickpeas provides a satisfying crunch, while a creamy avocado dip complements the snack, creating a balanced experience.

Another innovative product is his line of frozen desserts that utilize fruit purees and natural sweeteners. The interplay of creamy coconut milk with tangy passion fruit creates a delightful contrast, showcasing the beauty of flavor diversity. Each bite offers a different sensation, from the smoothness of the coconut to the burst of acidity from the fruit.

Challenges in Achieving Diversity

Despite the advancements in food technology, achieving diversity in textures and flavors presents challenges. One major issue is the balance between flavor intensity and texture integrity. For example, while adding flavor enhancers can elevate a dish, they may also alter the intended texture. Hernandez often experiments with ratios and cooking methods to find the perfect balance, ensuring that neither aspect overshadows the other.

Additionally, the sustainability of ingredients plays a crucial role in the diversity of flavors. Sourcing unique and diverse ingredients can be challenging, particularly in regions with limited access to global markets. Hernandez collaborates with local farmers and suppliers to source seasonal ingredients, promoting sustainability while enhancing the flavor profiles of his creations.

Conclusion

In conclusion, the diversity in textures and flavors is a cornerstone of Lee Hernandez's culinary philosophy. By embracing innovative techniques and thoughtful ingredient combinations, he has transformed the way we experience food. The interplay of textures and flavors not only enhances the sensory experience but also caters to the evolving needs of consumers, paving the way for a more inclusive and exciting culinary future. As Hernandez continues to push the boundaries of food technology, the exploration of diversity in textures and flavors will undoubtedly remain at the forefront of his culinary journey.

Creating products for different dietary needs

In today's diverse culinary landscape, the demand for food products that cater to various dietary needs has never been more pronounced. With rising awareness around health, allergies, and lifestyle choices, food innovators like Lee Hernandez have recognized the importance of inclusivity in food technology. This section explores the strategies employed by Culinary Innovations Inc. to develop products tailored for specific dietary requirements, as well as the underlying theories and challenges faced in this endeavor.

Understanding Dietary Needs

Dietary needs can be broadly categorized into several key areas, including but not limited to:

- **Allergies and Intolerances:** Common allergens such as gluten, nuts, dairy, and shellfish necessitate the creation of alternative products that maintain flavor and texture without compromising safety.

- **Health Conditions:** Individuals with diabetes, hypertension, or heart disease often require low-sugar, low-sodium, or heart-healthy options, respectively.

- **Lifestyle Choices:** Veganism, vegetarianism, and paleo diets are increasingly popular, prompting the need for products that align with these philosophies.

- **Age-Related Needs:** Older adults may benefit from products that are easier to chew and digest, as well as those fortified with essential nutrients.

Theoretical Frameworks

The development of food products for different dietary needs is rooted in several theoretical frameworks:

Nutritional Science   investigates the relationship between food components and health outcomes. Understanding macronutrients (proteins, fats, carbohydrates) and micronutrients (vitamins, minerals) is essential for creating balanced products. For instance, the formulation of a gluten-free bread requires a thorough understanding of how to replicate the structural properties of gluten using alternative ingredients such as almond flour or tapioca starch.

Sensory Evaluation   plays a crucial role in product development.   It involves assessing the sensory attributes of food, such as taste, texture, aroma, and appearance, which are vital for consumer acceptance. Techniques such as triangle tests and hedonic scaling allow innovators to refine their products until they meet consumer expectations.

Challenges in Product Development

Creating products that cater to different dietary needs presents several challenges:

+ **Ingredient Substitution:** Replacing traditional ingredients with alternatives can alter the final product's taste and texture. For example, substituting dairy with almond milk in ice cream may result in a different mouthfeel and flavor profile. Innovators must conduct extensive testing to find the right balance.

+ **Cross-Contamination:** For those with severe allergies, even trace amounts of allergens can pose significant health risks. Strict protocols must be implemented during production to prevent cross-contamination, which can complicate manufacturing processes.

+ **Consumer Education:** Many consumers may not fully understand the benefits or limitations of alternative products. Effective marketing and clear labeling are essential to inform potential customers about the dietary benefits and safety of the products.

Examples of Innovative Products

Culinary Innovations Inc. has successfully launched several products that cater to diverse dietary needs:

FlavorBurst™ Gluten-Free Pizza Crust   utilizes a blend of gluten-free flours and natural binders to create a crust that mimics the texture of traditional pizza. The product has been rigorously tested for taste and texture, receiving positive feedback from both gluten-sensitive consumers and pizza enthusiasts.

Plant-Based Protein Nuggets   target the growing vegan and vegetarian market. Made from pea protein, these nuggets provide a high-protein alternative to chicken nuggets, while also being free from common allergens. They are fortified with essential vitamins and minerals to ensure they meet the nutritional needs of individuals avoiding animal products.

Low-Sodium FlavorBurst™ Seasoning   caters to individuals with hypertension. By utilizing natural flavor enhancers such as herbs and spices, this product allows consumers to enjoy bold flavors without the health risks associated with high sodium intake.

Conclusion

The creation of food products that address different dietary needs is a complex yet rewarding challenge for innovators like Lee Hernandez. By leveraging nutritional science, sensory evaluation, and innovative ingredient sourcing, Culinary Innovations Inc. has positioned itself at the forefront of this culinary revolution. As consumer awareness and demand for tailored food products continue to grow, the commitment to inclusivity and health will remain a driving force in the future of food technology.

The global success of Culinary Innovations Inc.

Culinary Innovations Inc. emerged as a trailblazer in the food technology sector, quickly gaining recognition on a global scale. The company's success can be attributed to a combination of innovative product development, strategic marketing, and a commitment to addressing contemporary dietary needs. This section explores the factors contributing to the global success of Culinary Innovations Inc., the challenges encountered along the way, and the company's impact on the food industry.

Innovative Product Development

At the heart of Culinary Innovations Inc.'s success is its pioneering product line, which includes the groundbreaking FlavorBurst™. This product utilizes a proprietary technology that enhances flavor profiles through a unique combination of molecular gastronomy and food science. The equation governing the flavor enhancement can be expressed as:

$$F = \sum_{i=1}^{n}(A_i \cdot C_i)$$

where F represents the overall flavor intensity, A_i denotes the concentration of each flavor component, and C_i is the corresponding enhancement coefficient derived from culinary science experiments.   The meticulous research and development process behind FlavorBurst™ not only captivated consumers but also attracted the attention of food industry professionals worldwide.

Strategic Marketing and Brand Positioning

Culinary Innovations Inc. adopted a multifaceted marketing strategy that focused on positioning the brand as a leader in sustainable and innovative food solutions. The marketing team leveraged social media platforms, influencer partnerships, and targeted advertising campaigns to reach diverse audiences. A key aspect of their strategy was the emphasis on storytelling, highlighting the journey of Lee Hernandez and the mission behind the company.

The brand's unique value proposition—offering products that not only taste exceptional but also cater to various dietary restrictions—resonated with health-conscious consumers. For instance, the introduction of FlavorBurst™ in vegan and gluten-free variants expanded the market reach, tapping into the growing demand for inclusive food options.

Challenges and Solutions

Despite its rapid success, Culinary Innovations Inc. faced several challenges, including supply chain disruptions, skepticism from traditionalists in the culinary world, and the need to maintain consistent quality across global markets. To address these issues, the company implemented robust supply chain management practices, ensuring that ingredients were sourced sustainably and efficiently.

Moreover, to counter skepticism, Culinary Innovations Inc. invested in educational initiatives, conducting workshops and demonstrations that showcased the science behind their products. By engaging with chefs and culinary schools, they fostered a community of advocates who were willing to embrace innovative food technologies.

Global Expansion and Market Penetration

Culinary Innovations Inc. strategically entered international markets, adapting its product offerings to meet local tastes and preferences. For example, in Asian markets, the company introduced FlavorBurst™ variants that incorporated traditional spices and flavors, thereby appealing to regional palates. This localization strategy not only enhanced market penetration but also solidified the brand's reputation as a global innovator.

The success in international markets was further bolstered by partnerships with local distributors and retailers, facilitating widespread availability of Culinary

Innovations Inc.'s products. The company's ability to navigate diverse regulatory environments and cultural nuances played a crucial role in its global expansion efforts.

Impact on the Food Industry

The global success of Culinary Innovations Inc. has had a profound impact on the food industry, inspiring a new wave of culinary entrepreneurs to explore the intersection of food and technology. The company's emphasis on sustainability and innovation has prompted competitors to reevaluate their practices, leading to a broader industry shift toward environmentally responsible food production.

Furthermore, Culinary Innovations Inc.'s commitment to philanthropy, including partnerships with organizations focused on reducing food waste and promoting sustainable agriculture, has positioned the company as a leader in corporate social responsibility within the food sector.

Conclusion

In conclusion, the global success of Culinary Innovations Inc. can be attributed to its innovative product development, strategic marketing efforts, and commitment to sustainability. By addressing contemporary dietary needs and fostering a culture of culinary innovation, the company has not only carved a niche for itself in the food technology landscape but has also inspired a new generation of food innovators. As Culinary Innovations Inc. continues to evolve, its influence on the food industry will undoubtedly shape the future of culinary practices and consumer expectations worldwide.

Culinary Revolution: Transforming the Food Industry

Disruption and transformation

Embracing sustainability in food production

In recent years, the food industry has faced increasing scrutiny regarding its environmental impact. As the global population continues to rise, the demand for food is projected to increase by 70% by 2050 [?]. This surge in demand presents significant challenges, necessitating a shift towards sustainable food production practices. Sustainable food production aims to meet the needs of the present without compromising the ability of future generations to meet their own needs, aligning with the principles of sustainable development [?].

Theoretical Framework

Sustainability in food production can be understood through three interconnected pillars: environmental, economic, and social sustainability.

+ **Environmental Sustainability:** This aspect focuses on reducing the ecological footprint of food production. It involves practices that minimize resource depletion, reduce greenhouse gas emissions, and protect biodiversity [?].

+ **Economic Sustainability:** This dimension emphasizes the need for food systems to be economically viable. Producers must be able to generate enough income to sustain their operations while providing affordable food to consumers [?].

- **Social Sustainability:** Social sustainability addresses issues of equity, labor rights, and community well-being. It advocates for fair wages, safe working conditions, and the empowerment of local communities [?].

Problems in Current Food Production Systems

Despite the theoretical framework supporting sustainability, numerous problems persist in current food production systems:

- **Resource Depletion:** Conventional agricultural practices often lead to soil degradation, water scarcity, and loss of biodiversity. For instance, intensive farming can result in soil erosion rates exceeding natural replenishment, leading to a decline in soil fertility [?].

- **Greenhouse Gas Emissions:** The food sector contributes approximately 25% of global greenhouse gas emissions, predominantly from livestock production, deforestation for agriculture, and the use of synthetic fertilizers [?].

- **Food Waste:** Approximately one-third of all food produced globally is wasted, representing a significant waste of resources and contributing to environmental degradation [?].

Innovative Approaches to Sustainable Food Production

To address these challenges, innovators like Lee Hernandez are embracing various strategies to promote sustainability in food production:

- **Agroecology:** This approach integrates ecological principles into agricultural practices, promoting biodiversity and reducing reliance on chemical inputs. Agroecological practices, such as crop rotation and intercropping, enhance soil health and resilience [?].

- **Precision Agriculture:** Utilizing technology, precision agriculture involves monitoring and managing field variability to optimize inputs and minimize waste. For example, sensor technologies can provide real-time data on soil moisture levels, allowing farmers to apply water and nutrients more efficiently [?].

- **Vertical Farming:** As urbanization continues to rise, vertical farming presents a solution for producing food in urban environments. These systems utilize controlled environments and hydroponics to grow crops with minimal land use and reduced transportation emissions [?].

Case Studies and Examples

Several case studies exemplify the successful implementation of sustainable practices in food production:

- **The EAT-Lancet Commission:** This initiative emphasizes the need for a universal dietary guideline that promotes health while ensuring environmental sustainability. The commission's report outlines a planetary health diet that balances plant-based foods with limited animal products, significantly reducing the environmental impact of food systems [?].

- **Urban Agriculture Initiatives:** Cities like Detroit have embraced urban farming as a means to revitalize communities and provide fresh produce. Initiatives such as the Detroit Black Community Food Security Network empower local residents to grow their own food, addressing food deserts while fostering community resilience [?].

- **Sustainable Seafood Practices:** Organizations like the Marine Stewardship Council (MSC) promote sustainable fishing practices by certifying fisheries that adhere to environmentally responsible practices. This certification helps consumers make informed choices, supporting sustainable seafood production [?].

Conclusion

Embracing sustainability in food production is not merely an option but a necessity in the face of pressing global challenges. By integrating innovative practices and fostering collaboration among stakeholders, the food industry can transition towards a more sustainable future. Lee Hernandez's contributions to culinary technology exemplify how innovation can drive sustainability, ensuring that future generations can enjoy a diverse and healthy food system.

Reducing food waste through innovative solutions

Food waste is a pressing global issue, with approximately one-third of all food produced for human consumption lost or wasted each year, amounting to about 1.3 billion tonnes. This waste not only represents a significant loss of resources, including water, labor, and energy, but also contributes to greenhouse gas emissions, exacerbating climate change. The need for innovative solutions to reduce food waste has never been more critical. Lee Hernandez, through his culinary innovations, has been at the forefront of this movement, developing technologies and strategies that address the problem at its core.

Understanding the Problem

Food waste occurs at various stages of the supply chain, from production and processing to distribution and consumption. The reasons for food waste are multifaceted, including:

- **Overproduction:** Farmers often produce more food than the market can absorb to mitigate risks associated with crop failures or price fluctuations.

- **Cosmetic Standards:** Retailers frequently reject perfectly edible food that does not meet aesthetic standards, leading to significant waste.

- **Consumer Behavior:** Households often purchase more food than they can consume, leading to spoilage and disposal.

- **Lack of Awareness:** Many consumers are unaware of how to store food properly or use leftovers creatively.

To effectively combat food waste, innovative solutions must target these areas, leveraging technology and education to create a more sustainable food system.

Innovative Solutions

Lee Hernandez has pioneered several innovative solutions aimed at reducing food waste, focusing on technology, product development, and consumer education.

1. Smart Inventory Management One of the key areas in which technology can play a transformative role is in inventory management. By utilizing advanced analytics and machine learning algorithms, businesses can optimize their inventory levels and reduce overproduction. For example, Hernandez's Culinary Innovations Inc. developed a software platform that analyzes purchasing patterns and predicts demand more accurately. This system allows retailers to adjust their orders dynamically, minimizing excess stock.

$$\text{Optimal Order Quantity} = \sqrt{\frac{2DS}{H}} \tag{39}$$

Where:

+ D = Demand rate (units per time period)

+ S = Ordering cost per order

+ H = Holding cost per unit per time period

This formula helps businesses determine the optimal order quantity to reduce waste while meeting customer demand.

2. Upcycling Food Waste Hernandez has also championed the concept of upcycling food waste, transforming by-products and unsold food into new products. For instance, his team developed a line of sauces and condiments made from surplus fruits and vegetables that would otherwise go to waste. This not only reduces food waste but also creates new revenue streams for businesses.

Case Study: FlavorBurst™

A prime example of Hernandez's innovative approach is the creation of FlavorBurst™, a product designed to enhance the flavor of leftover ingredients. By using a proprietary process that concentrates flavors from food that would typically be discarded, FlavorBurst™ allows consumers to elevate their meals without generating additional waste.

3. Consumer Education and Engagement Beyond technological solutions, educating consumers about food waste is crucial. Hernandez has launched campaigns to raise awareness about proper food storage techniques and creative uses for leftovers. These initiatives encourage consumers to rethink their purchasing habits and reduce waste at home.

The Role of Collaboration

Addressing food waste effectively requires collaboration among various stakeholders, including farmers, retailers, food manufacturers, and consumers. Hernandez has established partnerships with local farms to create a closed-loop system where surplus produce is redirected to food banks or transformed into value-added products. This holistic approach not only reduces waste but also supports local communities.

Conclusion

Reducing food waste through innovative solutions is a critical component of creating a sustainable food system. Lee Hernandez's work exemplifies how technology, creative product development, and consumer education can work together to tackle this global challenge. By embracing these innovative strategies, we can significantly reduce food waste, conserve resources, and contribute to a healthier planet for future generations.

Collaborations with farmers and suppliers

In the rapidly evolving landscape of food technology, the collaboration between innovators like Lee Hernandez and local farmers and suppliers has emerged as a pivotal element in transforming the food industry. These partnerships not only enhance the quality and sustainability of food products but also contribute to a more resilient food system.

The Importance of Local Sourcing

Local sourcing is a critical aspect of modern culinary practices. By collaborating with local farmers, Lee Hernandez has been able to ensure that the ingredients used in his products are not only fresh but also sustainably grown. This approach reduces the carbon footprint associated with long-distance transportation and supports local economies.

$$\text{Carbon Footprint} = \text{Distance} \times \text{Weight} \times \text{Emission Factor} \qquad (40)$$

Where: - *Distance* is the distance traveled by the food product, - *Weight* is the weight of the food product, - *Emission Factor* is the average emissions produced per unit weight per distance traveled.

By minimizing the *Distance* in this equation, Hernandez not only lowers the overall *Carbon Footprint* but also promotes a sustainable model of food production.

Building Trust and Transparency

Collaborating with farmers fosters trust and transparency in the food supply chain. Hernandez emphasizes the importance of knowing the origins of his ingredients, which aligns with the growing consumer demand for transparency in food sourcing. By visiting farms, participating in harvests, and engaging directly with farmers, Hernandez can ensure that the ethical and environmental standards he values are upheld.

For example, when developing FlavorBurst™, Hernandez partnered with a local organic farm that specializes in heirloom vegetables. This collaboration allowed him to utilize unique flavor profiles that are not typically found in mass-produced ingredients, thereby enhancing the culinary experience for consumers.

Addressing Challenges in Food Production

Despite the benefits, collaborations with farmers are not without challenges. Issues such as seasonal availability, crop failures due to climate change, and fluctuating market prices can pose significant risks. To mitigate these challenges, Hernandez employs several strategies:

- **Diversification of Suppliers:** By working with multiple farmers, Hernandez can ensure a steady supply of ingredients even if one source encounters difficulties.

- **Seasonal Menu Planning:** Incorporating seasonal ingredients into product lines allows for flexibility and adaptability in the face of supply challenges.

- **Investment in Sustainable Practices:** Collaborating with farmers to implement sustainable agricultural practices not only improves crop resilience but also enhances the quality of the produce.

For instance, during a particularly harsh growing season, Hernandez's team worked closely with farmers to develop a contingency plan that included alternative crops and methods for extending the growing season, such as hoop houses and crop rotation strategies.

Innovative Partnerships for Sustainability

One of the most notable aspects of Hernandez's collaborations is his commitment to sustainability. By partnering with suppliers who prioritize eco-friendly practices, he has been able to create a supply chain that minimizes waste and promotes biodiversity.

For example, Hernandez collaborated with a local dairy farm that practices regenerative agriculture, which focuses on restoring soil health and enhancing biodiversity. This partnership not only provided high-quality dairy products for his innovations but also allowed Hernandez to actively participate in initiatives aimed at improving the overall health of the ecosystem.

Case Study: The Farm-to-Table Initiative

A prime example of Hernandez's successful collaborations is the Farm-to-Table initiative, which connects local farmers directly with consumers through community-supported agriculture (CSA) programs. This initiative has been instrumental in promoting local food systems and reducing food waste.

$$\text{Food Waste Reduction} = \text{Total Food Produced} - \text{Food Consumed} \tag{41}$$

The initiative has resulted in a significant reduction in food waste, as consumers are encouraged to purchase seasonal produce directly from farmers. Hernandez's role in this initiative has involved organizing workshops and events that educate consumers on the benefits of local sourcing and seasonal eating.

Conclusion

Collaborations with farmers and suppliers have proven to be a cornerstone of Lee Hernandez's approach to culinary innovation. By fostering relationships based on trust, sustainability, and shared values, he has not only enhanced the quality of his products but also contributed to a more resilient and ethical food system. As the food industry continues to evolve, these partnerships will be crucial in addressing the challenges of food production and ensuring a sustainable future for all.

Influencing new trends in food culture

Shaping the Future of Food Service

The landscape of food service is undergoing a seismic shift, driven by technological advancements and changing consumer preferences. Lee Hernandez, with his innovative approach, has played a pivotal role in this transformation, leveraging food technology to redefine how we experience dining.

The Rise of Technology in Food Service

The integration of technology in food service has become not just an enhancement but a necessity. From mobile ordering systems to automated kitchen equipment, the efficiency and convenience of technology have revolutionized the industry. According to a report by the National Restaurant Association, over 60% of consumers are interested in using technology to enhance their dining experience.

$$\text{Efficiency} = \frac{\text{Output}}{\text{Input}} \tag{42}$$

This equation underscores the importance of maximizing output while minimizing input, a principle that Lee Hernandez applies in his culinary innovations. For instance, the implementation of AI-driven inventory management systems allows restaurants to predict stock needs accurately, reducing waste and optimizing costs.

Personalization and Customization

Consumers today crave personalized experiences, and food service is no exception. Lee Hernandez's culinary innovations have emphasized customization, allowing customers to tailor their meals according to their preferences. This trend is supported by data indicating that 70% of diners are more likely to return to a restaurant that offers personalized menu options.

One example of this is the FlavorBurst™ product line, which allows diners to select specific flavor profiles and textures that suit their individual tastes. By utilizing data analytics, restaurants can track customer preferences and offer personalized recommendations, further enhancing the dining experience.

Sustainability in Food Service

As environmental concerns rise, sustainability has become a cornerstone of modern food service. Lee Hernandez champions sustainable practices by collaborating with local farmers and suppliers to source ingredients responsibly. This not only supports the local economy but also reduces the carbon footprint associated with food transportation.

$$\text{Sustainability Index} = \frac{\text{Local Sourcing} + \text{Waste Reduction}}{\text{Total Production}} \tag{43}$$

This equation illustrates the relationship between local sourcing, waste reduction, and overall sustainability in food service. By prioritizing these factors, establishments can enhance their sustainability index, appealing to environmentally-conscious consumers.

The Role of Fusion Cuisine

Fusion cuisine is another trend that Lee Hernandez has embraced, blending culinary traditions from various cultures to create unique dining experiences. This approach not only showcases diversity but also caters to the evolving palates of consumers seeking new flavors.

A notable example is the creation of dishes that combine traditional techniques from Asian cuisines with contemporary Western flavors. This not only attracts a broader audience but also encourages culinary experimentation, pushing the boundaries of what food can be.

Challenges in the Evolving Landscape

Despite the exciting possibilities, the evolution of food service is not without its challenges. One significant issue is the need for staff training in new technologies and culinary techniques. As kitchens become more automated, the workforce must adapt to these changes, requiring ongoing education and training programs.

Moreover, there is a risk of alienating traditionalists who may resist these innovations. Balancing innovation with the preservation of culinary heritage is crucial for maintaining a diverse food culture. Lee Hernandez addresses this challenge by incorporating traditional elements into his modern creations, ensuring that the essence of culinary arts is not lost.

Conclusion: A New Era in Food Service

In conclusion, the future of food service is being shaped by innovative thinkers like Lee Hernandez, who are redefining the dining experience through technology, personalization, sustainability, and fusion cuisine. As the industry continues to evolve, it is essential for food service professionals to embrace these changes while remaining true to the rich traditions that define culinary arts.

This dynamic landscape presents both opportunities and challenges, but with visionary leaders at the helm, the future of food service promises to be as exciting as it is delicious.

Fusion cuisine and the blending of cultures

Fusion cuisine represents a remarkable intersection of culinary traditions, where chefs and food innovators combine elements from different cultural backgrounds to create innovative dishes that challenge the norms of traditional gastronomy. This culinary movement not only reflects globalization but also celebrates diversity, allowing flavors and techniques from various regions to coexist harmoniously on a single plate.

Theoretical Framework of Fusion Cuisine

The concept of fusion cuisine can be understood through the lens of cultural hybridity, which posits that cultural identities are not fixed but rather fluid and constantly evolving. Homi K. Bhabha, a prominent cultural theorist, discusses the notion of the "third space," where cultural exchanges occur, resulting in new forms of identity and expression. In the culinary context, this "third space" is where diverse culinary practices meet, leading to the creation of unique flavor profiles and innovative cooking methods.

$$C = f(C_1, C_2, \ldots, C_n) \tag{44}$$

In this equation, C represents the resultant fusion cuisine, while $C_1, C_2, \ldots, C_n$ denote the various cultural influences being integrated. The function f signifies the creative process undertaken by chefs to merge these influences, resulting in a new culinary experience.

Challenges of Fusion Cuisine

Despite its appeal, fusion cuisine is not without its challenges. One significant issue is the potential for cultural appropriation, where elements of a culture are used without proper understanding or respect for their origins. This can lead to backlash from communities whose culinary traditions are being represented. For instance, the use of traditional Asian ingredients in a Western-style dish may be seen as a commodification of those cultural elements, stripping them of their significance and context.

Additionally, there is the risk of creating dishes that lack authenticity or coherence. When blending multiple culinary traditions, there is a fine line between innovation and confusion. Chefs must navigate the delicate balance of respecting the integrity of each cuisine while also pushing the boundaries of creativity. A poorly executed fusion dish can result in an unpalatable combination, leading to customer dissatisfaction and criticism.

Examples of Successful Fusion Cuisine

Several chefs have successfully embraced fusion cuisine, creating dishes that celebrate the blending of cultures while maintaining respect for their origins. One notable example is the work of Chef Roy Choi, who gained fame for his Korean-Mexican taco truck, Kogi BBQ. His signature dish, the Korean BBQ taco, combines marinated short ribs, fresh cilantro, and spicy kimchi, wrapped in a soft tortilla. This dish not only highlights the flavors of both cuisines but also reflects the cultural melting pot of Los Angeles, where Choi operates.

Another exemplary figure in the fusion cuisine landscape is Chef Nobu Matsuhisa, who has popularized the concept of Nikkei cuisine—a blend of Japanese and Peruvian flavors. His signature dish, Black Cod Miso, showcases the harmonious marriage of miso-marinated black cod with traditional Peruvian ingredients, exemplifying how culinary techniques and flavors can transcend cultural boundaries.

The Future of Fusion Cuisine

As globalization continues to shape the culinary landscape, fusion cuisine is poised to evolve further. The increasing accessibility of global ingredients and culinary techniques allows chefs to experiment with combinations that were previously unimaginable. Moreover, the rise of social media has enabled food lovers to share their culinary experiences, fostering a culture of experimentation and creativity.

In the future, we may witness the emergence of new fusion trends that incorporate not only traditional cuisines but also modern dietary preferences, such as plant-based and gluten-free options. As consumers become more health-conscious, the integration of diverse culinary traditions with innovative health-oriented practices will likely become a focal point in the evolution of fusion cuisine.

Conclusion

Fusion cuisine embodies the spirit of culinary innovation, showcasing the beauty of cultural exchange and the endless possibilities that arise when diverse culinary traditions come together. By respecting the origins of the ingredients and techniques used, chefs can create dishes that not only tantalize the taste buds but also tell a story of cultural connection and collaboration. As we look to the future, the blending of cultures in the culinary world will continue to inspire new generations of chefs and food enthusiasts, paving the way for a more inclusive and diverse food landscape.

Inspiring a new generation of food entrepreneurs

In the rapidly evolving landscape of the culinary arts, Lee Hernandez stands as a beacon of inspiration for aspiring food entrepreneurs. His journey exemplifies the fusion of creativity, technology, and business acumen, encouraging a new generation to embrace innovation in the food industry. This section explores the ways in which

Hernandez has influenced emerging culinary talents, the challenges they face, and the vital role of mentorship in fostering the next wave of food innovators.

The Importance of Innovation in Food Entrepreneurship

The food industry is at a critical juncture, driven by changing consumer preferences, technological advancements, and sustainability concerns. Young entrepreneurs must navigate these complexities while carving out their unique niches. According to a report by the Food and Agriculture Organization (FAO), *"Innovation in food systems is essential to meet the growing global demand for food while ensuring environmental sustainability."* This statement underscores the necessity for fresh ideas and approaches in food production, distribution, and consumption.

Hernandez's pioneering work in food technology, particularly with his FlavorBurst™ product, serves as a case study for aspiring entrepreneurs. By merging culinary artistry with scientific principles, he demonstrates how innovation can lead to the creation of products that not only tantalize the palate but also address broader issues such as sustainability and health. This approach encourages young chefs and food technologists to think outside the box and to consider how their innovations can contribute positively to society.

Challenges Faced by Aspiring Food Entrepreneurs

Despite the opportunities presented by the modern food landscape, aspiring entrepreneurs encounter significant challenges. These include:

+ **Market Saturation:** The food industry is highly competitive, with countless new products and concepts emerging daily. Standing out requires not only creativity but also a deep understanding of market trends and consumer behavior.

+ **Access to Funding:** Securing capital for food startups can be daunting. Many entrepreneurs struggle to find investors who believe in their vision, especially in an industry where traditional funding avenues may overlook innovative food tech solutions.

+ **Regulatory Hurdles:** Navigating food safety regulations and compliance can be complex, particularly for those introducing novel ingredients or technologies. Entrepreneurs must be well-versed in the legal landscape to avoid costly setbacks.

These challenges can be daunting, but they also present opportunities for growth and learning. Hernandez's story illustrates how perseverance and adaptability are key traits for success in this dynamic environment.

The Role of Mentorship in Nurturing New Talent

One of the most significant ways Hernandez inspires the next generation is through mentorship. He actively engages with young chefs and food entrepreneurs, sharing his insights and experiences. Research indicates that mentorship can significantly enhance an entrepreneur's chances of success. According to a study published in the *Journal of Business Venturing*, mentees are more likely to secure funding, develop viable business plans, and navigate challenges effectively when guided by experienced mentors.

Hernandez's mentorship extends beyond personal interactions; he has established programs and workshops aimed at equipping aspiring food entrepreneurs with the skills they need to thrive. These initiatives focus on:

- **Business Acumen:** Teaching young innovators about the fundamentals of running a successful food business, including financial management, marketing strategies, and supply chain logistics.

- **Technical Skills:** Providing hands-on training in food technology and culinary techniques, enabling participants to experiment with new ideas and develop their own unique products.

- **Networking Opportunities:** Connecting emerging entrepreneurs with industry professionals, investors, and potential collaborators, fostering a supportive community that encourages innovation.

Case Studies of Inspired Entrepreneurs

Several young entrepreneurs have emerged as a result of Hernandez's influence, showcasing the potential of innovative thinking in the culinary arts. For instance, Sarah Kim, a protégé of Hernandez, launched *EcoEats*, a sustainable meal kit service that focuses on zero-waste cooking. By utilizing local produce and minimizing packaging, Kim's venture not only addresses environmental concerns but also caters to health-conscious consumers.

Another example is Jamal Patel, who developed a line of plant-based snacks inspired by traditional recipes from his heritage. With Hernandez's guidance, Patel was able to refine his product and secure funding, leading to a successful launch that has garnered attention for its cultural significance and innovative approach to snacking.

These examples illustrate the ripple effect of Hernandez's mentorship, as each new entrepreneur carries forward the lessons learned and the spirit of innovation, further enriching the culinary landscape.

Conclusion: A Legacy of Inspiration

Lee Hernandez's commitment to inspiring a new generation of food entrepreneurs is a testament to his belief in the power of innovation and collaboration. By sharing his knowledge, experiences, and resources, he not only empowers young chefs to pursue their dreams but also fosters a culture of creativity and sustainability within the food industry.

As the culinary world continues to evolve, the impact of Hernandez's mentorship will undoubtedly resonate for years to come. The next wave of food innovators, equipped with the tools and inspiration provided by Hernandez, will play a crucial role in shaping the future of food, ensuring that it is not only delicious but also sustainable and inclusive.

In summary, the journey of aspiring food entrepreneurs is fraught with challenges, yet it is also filled with opportunities for growth and innovation. With mentors like Lee Hernandez leading the way, the future of food entrepreneurship looks bright, promising a new era of culinary creativity that will inspire generations to come.

Personal Life: Balancing Passion and Relationships

The challenges of success

Personal sacrifices and hectic schedules

The journey of Lee Hernandez, a culinary innovator, is not without its share of personal sacrifices and the challenges of maintaining a hectic schedule. As he climbed the ranks of the food technology industry, the demands of his career often came at the expense of personal time and relationships. This section delves into the complexities of balancing a thriving career with personal commitments, highlighting the struggles and strategies that accompany such a high-paced lifestyle.

The Cost of Ambition

Ambition is a double-edged sword. While it drives individuals to achieve greatness, it often demands sacrifices that can take a toll on personal lives. For Lee, the relentless pursuit of culinary innovation meant long hours in the lab and the kitchen. The equation that often defined his life can be summarized as follows:

$$\text{Success} = \text{Time Invested} + \text{Opportunities Seized} - \text{Personal Sacrifices} \quad (45)$$

This equation reflects the reality that the more time Lee invested in his work, the more opportunities he could seize, yet it also meant that personal sacrifices became an inevitable part of his journey. Family gatherings, friends' events, and even personal hobbies were frequently sidelined as he focused on developing groundbreaking food technologies.

Hectic Schedules and Time Management

Lee's typical day was a whirlwind of activities, often beginning before dawn and extending late into the night. Managing such a hectic schedule required exceptional time management skills. He utilized various strategies, such as prioritizing tasks, delegating responsibilities, and employing technology to streamline processes.

One effective method Lee adopted was the Eisenhower Matrix, which categorizes tasks based on urgency and importance. This allowed him to focus on what truly mattered, ensuring that critical projects received the attention they required while less urgent tasks could be postponed or delegated.

$$\text{Eisenhower Matrix} = \begin{cases} \text{Urgent and Important\&} \Rightarrow \text{Do it now} \\ \text{Important, not Urgent\&} \Rightarrow \text{Schedule it} \\ \text{Urgent, not Important\&} \Rightarrow \text{Delegate it} \\ \text{Not Urgent, not Important\&} \Rightarrow \text{Eliminate it} \end{cases} \quad (46)$$

Despite these strategies, Lee often found himself stretched thin, grappling with the mental and emotional toll of his commitments. The constant juggling act left little room for spontaneity or relaxation, leading to feelings of burnout.

Impact on Relationships

The sacrifices made in pursuit of success inevitably affected Lee's relationships. Friends and family often felt neglected, and the strain on personal connections became increasingly apparent. Lee's partner, who initially admired his passion, began to express concerns about the time he spent away from home.

In a candid moment, Lee reflected on the impact of his career on his relationship, stating, "I realized that while I was busy building my empire, I was also building walls around my personal life." This acknowledgment forced him to reassess his priorities, leading to a more intentional approach to nurturing his relationships.

Finding Balance

Recognizing the need for balance, Lee implemented several strategies to reconnect with his loved ones. He scheduled regular date nights with his partner and made a conscious effort to attend family gatherings, even if it meant stepping away from work for a few hours.

Additionally, Lee began to incorporate mindfulness practices into his routine, such as meditation and yoga, which helped him manage stress and maintain focus.

By prioritizing self-care, he found that he could approach his work with renewed energy and creativity.

Conclusion

In conclusion, the path to success in the culinary world is fraught with personal sacrifices and the challenges of managing a hectic schedule. Lee Hernandez's journey serves as a reminder that while ambition can drive innovation, it is essential to strike a balance between professional aspirations and personal well-being. By learning to navigate these challenges, Lee not only found success in his career but also reconnected with the relationships that matter most, ultimately enriching both his personal and professional life.

Maintaining relationships in a fast-paced industry

In the culinary world, particularly within the realm of food technology, maintaining personal relationships can be a formidable challenge. The fast-paced nature of the industry often demands long hours, intense focus, and a relentless pursuit of innovation. For Lee Hernandez, navigating the complexities of personal connections while establishing a thriving career became a critical aspect of his journey.

Theoretical Framework

Theories of work-life balance provide a useful lens through which to examine the relationship dynamics faced by professionals in high-demand fields. According to the *Work-Family Conflict Theory*, individuals experience conflict when the demands of work interfere with family responsibilities and vice versa. This theory emphasizes the importance of resources—both personal and organizational—that can mitigate conflict and facilitate balance.

Mathematically, this can be expressed as:

$$WFC = f(WD, FD) \tag{47}$$

Where WFC is work-family conflict, WD is work demands, and FD is family demands. As work demands increase, the potential for conflict escalates, necessitating strategies to maintain harmony between professional aspirations and personal relationships.

Challenges Faced by Lee Hernandez

Lee's ascent in the culinary technology sector was marked by numerous challenges that tested his ability to maintain relationships. The demands of his role at Culinary Innovations Inc. often required him to work late nights and weekends, leading to missed family gatherings and important milestones.

For instance, during the launch of FlavorBurst™, Lee found himself preoccupied with product testing and marketing strategies, which resulted in him missing his daughter's first school play. This incident highlighted the emotional toll that professional obligations can impose on personal life.

Strategies for Relationship Maintenance

To counteract the pressures of his career, Lee implemented several strategies that allowed him to nurture his relationships without compromising his professional goals:

- **Scheduled Quality Time:** Lee made it a priority to schedule regular family dinners and weekend outings. By carving out dedicated time for loved ones, he ensured that his relationships remained a focal point amidst his busy schedule.

- **Open Communication:** Lee practiced transparency with his family about his work commitments. By sharing his schedule and discussing upcoming projects, he fostered understanding and patience among his loved ones, which helped alleviate feelings of neglect.

- **Involvement in Family Activities:** Lee sought opportunities to involve his family in his culinary world. Whether it was hosting cooking sessions at home or inviting them to product launches, this approach helped bridge the gap between his professional and personal life, creating shared experiences.

- **Mindfulness Practices:** To manage stress and maintain emotional connections, Lee adopted mindfulness techniques. Regular meditation and reflection allowed him to remain present during family interactions, enhancing the quality of time spent together.

Examples of Success

The effectiveness of Lee's strategies became evident over time. By prioritizing family engagement, he was able to attend his daughter's next school play, where he not only cheered her on but also connected with other parents, strengthening his social network outside of work.

Moreover, during a particularly demanding project, Lee's family organized a surprise dinner to celebrate his efforts. This gesture not only reaffirmed their support but also motivated Lee to continue balancing his commitments.

Conclusion

In conclusion, maintaining relationships in a fast-paced culinary industry requires intentional effort and strategic planning. Lee Hernandez's journey illustrates that while the demands of innovation and entrepreneurship can be overwhelming, prioritizing personal connections is essential for long-term success and fulfillment. By employing effective strategies and fostering open communication, Lee was able to navigate the complexities of his professional life while nurturing the relationships that mattered most. Ultimately, the balance he achieved not only enriched his personal life but also contributed positively to his professional endeavors, demonstrating that success is not solely measured by achievements but also by the quality of the connections we cultivate along the way.

Struggles with work-life balance

In the fast-paced world of culinary innovation, achieving a work-life balance can be a daunting challenge, especially for someone like Lee Hernandez, whose passion for food technology often blurs the lines between personal and professional life. The high demands of the culinary industry, coupled with the entrepreneurial responsibilities of running a successful startup, can lead to significant stress and personal sacrifices.

Theories of work-life balance suggest that individuals often strive to manage their time and energy between work commitments and personal life. According to Greenhaus and Allen (2011), work-life balance is defined as "the extent to which an individual is engaged in and enjoys their work role and their family role." This balance is crucial for overall well-being, yet it remains elusive for many professionals, particularly in high-stakes fields like culinary arts.

For Lee, the early stages of his career were marked by long hours and relentless pursuit of excellence. The pressure to innovate and produce groundbreaking culinary products often meant that workdays stretched into nights, leaving little time for personal relationships or self-care. Lee recalls, "There were nights I would come home after a 14-hour shift, too exhausted to even eat. I realized I was missing out on important moments with my family."

The Cost of Ambition

One of the primary problems that Lee faced was the expectation of constant availability. In the culinary world, trends shift rapidly, and staying ahead requires not just dedication but also an unyielding commitment. This often led to feelings of guilt when he took time off or prioritized personal matters over work. A study by Kahn and Byosiere (1992) highlights that individuals in high-demand roles frequently experience "role conflict," where the expectations of one role can negatively impact another. For Lee, this manifested in missed family events and strained relationships with friends.

Moreover, the entrepreneurial aspect of Lee's career introduced additional layers of complexity. As the founder of Culinary Innovations Inc., he felt the weight of responsibility not only for his work but also for his employees and stakeholders. This sense of duty often led to a cycle of overwork, where the fear of failure overshadowed the importance of personal well-being. Lee reflected, "I was so focused on building my empire that I forgot to take care of myself. I thought success meant sacrificing everything else."

Practical Strategies for Balance

To combat these struggles, Lee sought to implement practical strategies aimed at improving his work-life balance. One approach he adopted was the establishment of clear boundaries between work and personal time. He began to schedule "no work" hours in his calendar, during which he would focus solely on family and self-care. Research by Kossek and Ozeki (1998) supports the effectiveness of such boundary management strategies, indicating that they can lead to reduced stress and increased job satisfaction.

Additionally, Lee recognized the importance of delegation. As his company grew, he learned to trust his team and delegate responsibilities, allowing him to step back from day-to-day operations and focus on strategic decisions. This shift not only alleviated his workload but also empowered his employees, fostering a collaborative work environment. "I realized that I didn't have to do everything myself. Trusting my team was a game changer," he noted.

The Ongoing Journey

Despite these efforts, the struggle for balance remains an ongoing journey for Lee. He acknowledges that there are still days when work demands threaten to encroach on his personal life. However, through mindfulness practices and prioritizing self-care, he continues to strive for a healthier equilibrium. Mindfulness, as defined by Kabat-Zinn (1990), involves maintaining a moment-by-moment awareness of thoughts, feelings, and bodily sensations, which can be particularly beneficial in managing stress.

In conclusion, Lee Hernandez's journey illustrates the complexities of maintaining work-life balance in the culinary industry. While the pursuit of innovation and success can lead to personal sacrifices, implementing strategies such as boundary setting, delegation, and mindfulness can help mitigate these challenges. As Lee continues to evolve as both a culinary innovator and a family man, he remains committed to finding a balance that honors both his professional ambitions and personal life.

Love and family

Meeting the love of his life

Lee Hernandez's journey into the culinary world was not just marked by his professional milestones but also by the personal relationships he nurtured along the way. It was during his time at the prestigious Institute of Culinary Arts that he met the love of his life, Sofia Ramirez, a fellow culinary student with a passion for baking that rivaled his own enthusiasm for food technology.

A Fateful Encounter

Their first meeting took place in a bustling kitchen during a collaborative project. The task was to create a dish that combined both molecular gastronomy and traditional baking techniques. Lee, with his experimental mindset, was eager to push the boundaries of flavor, while Sofia brought a sense of creativity and precision to the table. As they worked together, their contrasting styles complemented each other beautifully, sparking not only a culinary partnership but also a romantic connection.

$$Culinary\ Chemistry = Creativity + Collaboration \qquad (48)$$

This equation captures the essence of their relationship. Their shared passion for food acted as a catalyst, igniting a flame that would grow stronger with each passing day. They spent long hours in the kitchen, experimenting with flavors, sharing dreams, and supporting one another through the rigors of culinary school.

Shared Values and Aspirations

As their relationship blossomed, Lee and Sofia discovered that they shared more than just a love for food. Both were deeply committed to sustainability and innovation in the culinary arts. They discussed the importance of reducing food waste and creating dishes that not only delighted the palate but also respected the environment. This shared vision laid the foundation for their future endeavors.

$$\text{Sustainable Cuisine} = \text{Innovative Techniques} + \text{Respect for Ingredients} \quad (49)$$

Their commitment to sustainability would later influence Lee's entrepreneurial ventures, as he sought to create products that aligned with their shared values. They often collaborated on projects that explored the intersection of technology and traditional cooking methods, leading to groundbreaking ideas that would shape their careers.

Navigating Challenges

However, the path of love was not without its challenges. As Lee's career began to take off, the demands of his burgeoning food technology startup often clashed with their personal time. The couple faced the struggle of maintaining their relationship amidst the whirlwind of success and ambition. Sofia, understanding yet yearning for more time together, often found herself at the crossroads of support and personal sacrifice.

$$\text{Work-Life Balance} = \frac{\text{Quality Time}}{\text{Career Demands}} \quad (50)$$

This equation highlighted the delicate balance they needed to achieve. They learned to prioritize their relationship, carving out dedicated time for each other despite their busy schedules. Date nights became sacred rituals, where they would explore new culinary experiences together, reigniting their passion for both food and each other.

A Culinary Partnership

As Lee's culinary empire grew, so did Sofia's career as a renowned pastry chef. Their partnership evolved into a dynamic collaboration, where they combined their expertise to create unique dining experiences. Together, they opened a pop-up restaurant that showcased their innovative dishes, attracting food enthusiasts and critics alike.

Their restaurant, aptly named *Fusion Flavors*, became a testament to their love story—each dish representing a chapter of their lives together. From savory entrees that highlighted Lee's food technology innovations to decadent desserts crafted by Sofia, every plate told a story of collaboration and love.

Building a Family

In time, Lee and Sofia decided to take their partnership to the next level by starting a family. They welcomed two children, who became the center of their world. Balancing the demands of parenthood with their professional aspirations was a challenge, but they approached it with the same creativity and teamwork that had defined their relationship from the beginning.

$$Family = Love + Shared\ Dreams \tag{51}$$

This equation encapsulated their approach to parenting. They instilled in their children a love for food, teaching them the importance of healthy eating, sustainability, and the joy of cooking together. Family cooking nights became a cherished tradition, where laughter and creativity filled their kitchen.

Conclusion

The love story of Lee Hernandez and Sofia Ramirez is a testament to the power of shared passions and mutual support. Through the challenges and triumphs of their culinary journeys, they built a life filled with love, innovation, and a commitment to making the world a better place through food. Their relationship not only enriched their personal lives but also fueled their professional aspirations, paving the way for a legacy that would inspire future generations of food innovators.

In the end, Lee's journey was not just about culinary achievements; it was about the love that nourished his soul and inspired his work. Together, they created a beautiful recipe for life—one that blended passion, creativity, and unwavering support.

Nurturing a supportive partnership

In the fast-paced world of culinary innovation, nurturing a supportive partnership becomes essential for maintaining both personal happiness and professional success. Lee Hernandez, while building his food empire, found a significant ally in his partner, who not only understood the demands of his career but also actively contributed to his journey.

The Importance of Mutual Support

A supportive partnership is characterized by mutual respect, understanding, and shared goals. Research in relationship psychology suggests that couples who engage in supportive behaviors tend to experience higher levels of relationship satisfaction and lower levels of stress. For Lee, having a partner who celebrated his achievements and provided emotional support during setbacks was crucial.

$$S = \frac{R + U}{2} \tag{52}$$

Where:

+ S = Support in the partnership

+ R = Respect for each other's careers

+ U = Understanding of personal challenges

In Lee's case, his partner not only respected his culinary ambitions but also understood the long hours and the emotional toll that came with them. This mutual understanding helped them navigate the complexities of their lives together.

Effective Communication

Effective communication is another cornerstone of a supportive partnership. Lee and his partner established open lines of dialogue about their feelings, expectations, and aspirations. This included discussing the pressures of Lee's career and how they could support each other through these challenges.

$$C = \frac{E + A + F}{3} \tag{53}$$

Where:

+ C = Communication effectiveness

+ E = Expression of feelings

+ A = Active listening

+ F = Frequency of discussions

Lee's partner practiced active listening, ensuring that Lee felt heard and valued. This not only strengthened their bond but also provided Lee with a safe space to express his fears and aspirations, ultimately enhancing his creativity and focus in his culinary pursuits.

Shared Goals and Values

Having shared goals and values is vital for a supportive partnership. Lee and his partner aligned their visions for the future, which included aspirations for family life, professional growth, and community engagement. They often discussed how they could integrate their individual goals to create a harmonious life together.

$$G = \frac{P + C}{2} \tag{54}$$

Where:

- G = Shared goals

- P = Personal aspirations

- C = Common interests

By fostering a sense of teamwork, they were able to celebrate each other's successes as if they were their own. For instance, when Lee received a prestigious award, his partner organized a surprise celebration to honor his hard work, reinforcing their commitment to each other's achievements.

Balancing Personal and Professional Life

The culinary industry is notorious for its demanding hours, often leading to burnout and stress. Lee recognized the importance of balancing his professional commitments with personal life. He and his partner made a conscious effort to set boundaries around work hours, ensuring they spent quality time together.

$$B = T - W \tag{55}$$

Where:

- B = Balance in life

- T = Time allocated for personal relationships

- W = Work commitments

They scheduled regular date nights and weekend getaways, which allowed them to reconnect and recharge. This balance not only strengthened their relationship but also enhanced Lee's productivity and creativity in his culinary endeavors.

Navigating Challenges Together

Every relationship faces challenges, and Lee's partnership was no exception. The pressures of the culinary world often led to stress and misunderstandings. However, Lee and his partner approached these challenges as a team. They employed problem-solving techniques to address issues as they arose, rather than letting them fester.

$$R = \frac{C + P}{2} \tag{56}$$

Where:

+ R = Relationship resilience

+ C = Communication during conflicts

+ P = Problem-solving strategies

For example, during a particularly demanding project launch, Lee felt overwhelmed and began to withdraw. His partner recognized the signs and initiated a conversation, allowing Lee to express his feelings and frustrations. Together, they devised a plan to manage the workload more effectively, demonstrating their commitment to each other's well-being.

Celebrating Each Other's Successes

In a supportive partnership, celebrating each other's successes is essential. Lee's partner made it a point to acknowledge not just the big milestones but also the small victories. This practice fostered an environment of encouragement and positivity.

$$E = \frac{S + A}{2} \tag{57}$$

Where:

+ E = Encouragement level

+ S = Shared celebrations

+ A = Acknowledgment of efforts

Lee often found motivation in his partner's enthusiasm for his work, which fueled his passion for culinary innovation. Whether it was a simple congratulatory note or a surprise dinner to celebrate a successful product launch, these gestures reinforced their bond and commitment to each other's dreams.

Conclusion

Nurturing a supportive partnership requires intentional effort, effective communication, and a shared vision for the future. Lee Hernandez's journey illustrates the profound impact that a loving and understanding partner can have on personal and professional success. By prioritizing their relationship amidst the demands of the culinary world, Lee and his partner created a strong foundation that allowed both to thrive, proving that love and innovation can indeed go hand in hand.

Raising a family amidst a culinary empire

Lee Hernandez's journey through the culinary world was not just about personal success; it was also about nurturing a family in the midst of a rapidly expanding culinary empire. Balancing the demands of a high-stakes career with the responsibilities of parenthood posed unique challenges that required both innovative thinking and strategic planning.

The Challenge of Time Management

As the founder of Culinary Innovations Inc., Lee's days were often filled with meetings, product development sessions, and industry events. The challenge of time management became paramount. Research indicates that effective time management is crucial for maintaining a healthy work-life balance. According to Covey's Time Management Matrix, prioritizing tasks based on urgency and importance can lead to better outcomes both professionally and personally [?].

Lee adopted this framework by categorizing his responsibilities into four quadrants:

Quadrant I: Important and UrgentQuadrant II: Important but Not UrgentQuadrant III: N

(58)

By focusing on Quadrant II, which includes family time and personal growth, Lee was able to carve out moments for his loved ones amidst a busy schedule.

Creating Family Traditions

To ensure that family remained a priority, Lee and his partner established traditions that brought everyone together. Weekly family dinners became a staple, where the family would gather to cook and share stories. These moments not only reinforced family bonds but also allowed Lee to pass down culinary skills and knowledge to his children. Research shows that family meals are linked to numerous benefits, including improved communication and stronger family relationships [?].

Lee often involved his children in the cooking process, teaching them about flavors, ingredients, and the importance of sustainability. This hands-on approach not only fostered a love for food but also instilled values of creativity and responsibility. For example, they would experiment with plant-based recipes, exploring the science of flavor combinations, which mirrored Lee's own journey into food technology.

Navigating the Pressures of Success

While Lee's culinary empire flourished, the pressures of success often weighed heavily on the family. The constant demand for innovation and the need to stay relevant in a competitive industry led to moments of stress. A study by the American Psychological Association highlights that high-achieving individuals often experience heightened stress levels, which can spill over into personal relationships [?].

To combat this, Lee and his partner implemented strategies to manage stress. They practiced mindfulness techniques, such as meditation and yoga, which helped them remain grounded. Additionally, they scheduled regular family retreats, allowing them to disconnect from work and reconnect with each other. These retreats provided a much-needed respite from the pressures of the culinary world, fostering a sense of unity and relaxation.

The Role of Support Systems

Support systems played a crucial role in Lee's ability to raise a family while managing a culinary empire. Both Lee and his partner recognized the importance of seeking help when needed. They enlisted the support of family members and friends who could assist with childcare, allowing them to focus on their careers without compromising their children's well-being.

Moreover, Lee's team at Culinary Innovations Inc. was not just a group of employees; they were like an extended family. By fostering a collaborative and supportive work environment, Lee created a culture where team members understood the importance of work-life balance. This culture allowed Lee to take necessary breaks without feeling guilty, knowing that his team was capable of maintaining the momentum of the business.

Lessons Learned and Future Aspirations

Through the challenges of raising a family amidst a culinary empire, Lee learned invaluable lessons about the importance of prioritizing relationships and nurturing connections. He often reflected on the balance between ambition and family, recognizing that true success is not solely measured by professional achievements but also by the quality of personal relationships.

As Lee looked to the future, he aspired to create a legacy that extended beyond his culinary innovations. He envisioned a world where future generations could appreciate the art of cooking and the significance of family meals. By establishing scholarships for aspiring chefs and supporting community initiatives, Lee aimed to inspire others to pursue their culinary passions while cherishing their familial bonds.

In conclusion, raising a family amidst a culinary empire was a journey filled with challenges and triumphs. Lee Hernandez's commitment to balancing his professional aspirations with his responsibilities as a parent exemplifies the notion that success is not just about personal accomplishments but also about fostering love, creativity, and togetherness within the family unit.

Achievements and Awards: Celebrating Success

Recognitions and honors

James Beard Foundation Awards

The James Beard Foundation Awards are often referred to as the "Oscars of the food world," recognizing outstanding chefs, restaurants, and culinary professionals in the United States. Established in 1990, these awards honor the legacy of James Beard, a renowned chef, cookbook author, and food writer who is often considered the father of American gastronomy. The awards celebrate excellence in various categories, including Best Chef, Best New Restaurant, and Outstanding Chef, among others.

Significance of the Awards

Winning a James Beard Award is a prestigious accolade that can significantly enhance a chef's or a restaurant's reputation. The recognition not only brings national attention but also elevates the standards of culinary arts in the country. The awards are judged by a panel of culinary experts, food critics, and previous winners, ensuring a rigorous selection process that highlights true excellence in the industry.

Lee Hernandez's Journey to the Awards

Lee Hernandez's culinary journey is marked by his relentless pursuit of innovation and excellence, which ultimately led him to be a recipient of the James Beard Foundation Awards. His first nomination came shortly after the launch of Culinary Innovations Inc., where he introduced his groundbreaking product,

FlavorBurst™. The product was revolutionary, utilizing advanced food technology to create a burst of flavor that enhanced dishes without compromising nutritional value.

The Impact of FlavorBurst™ on the Industry

FlavorBurst™ not only garnered attention for its unique taste but also for its potential in addressing dietary concerns. By incorporating natural ingredients and innovative techniques, Hernandez demonstrated that food technology could play a crucial role in modern culinary practices. The product's success led to Hernandez being nominated for the James Beard Award for Best New Product, a category that recognizes innovative food products that have made a significant impact on the culinary landscape.

Challenges Faced in the Award Process

While the journey to the James Beard Foundation Awards is often filled with excitement, it is not without its challenges. Hernandez faced skepticism from traditionalists within the culinary community, who were hesitant to embrace food technology. Critics questioned the authenticity of his creations, arguing that innovation could overshadow the essence of cooking. Despite these challenges, Hernandez remained steadfast, focusing on the quality and integrity of his products.

Recognition and Achievement

In 2023, Lee Hernandez was awarded the James Beard Award for Outstanding Chef, a testament to his contributions to the culinary world. This honor was not just a personal achievement but also a recognition of the potential of food technology to transform the industry. Hernandez's acceptance speech highlighted the importance of innovation in culinary arts and encouraged fellow chefs to embrace change and experimentation.

Celebrating Diversity in Culinary Arts

Hernandez's win also underscored the importance of diversity in the culinary arts. As a chef of Latino heritage, he emphasized the need for representation within the industry. His success story serves as an inspiration for aspiring chefs from diverse backgrounds, encouraging them to pursue their culinary dreams and challenge the status quo.

Conclusion

The James Beard Foundation Awards are more than just accolades; they represent a commitment to excellence and innovation in the culinary arts. For Lee Hernandez, receiving this prestigious award was a culmination of years of hard work, creativity, and a passion for food technology. His journey serves as a beacon for future innovators in the culinary world, illustrating that with dedication and vision, one can leave a lasting impact on the industry.

$$\text{Impact} = \text{Innovation} + \text{Quality} + \text{Representation} \qquad (59)$$

In this equation, the impact of a culinary innovator like Lee Hernandez is derived from a combination of innovation in food technology, the quality of the products, and the representation of diverse voices in the culinary landscape. The James Beard Foundation Awards celebrate this multifaceted approach to culinary excellence, paving the way for future generations of chefs and innovators.

Michelin Stars and International Acclaim

The Michelin Guide, originally conceived as a promotional tool for the Michelin tire company, has evolved into one of the most prestigious accolades in the culinary world. Awarding stars to restaurants is a rigorous process that evaluates the quality of food, mastery of technique, personality of the chef in the cuisine, value for money, and consistency over time. For Lee Hernandez, receiving Michelin stars has not only been a personal achievement but also a significant milestone in his career, propelling him to international acclaim.

The Significance of Michelin Stars

Michelin stars are awarded on a scale of one to three, with each level representing a different degree of culinary excellence:

- **One Star:** A very good restaurant in its category.
- **Two Stars:** Excellent cooking that is worth a detour.
- **Three Stars:** Exceptional cuisine that is worth a special journey.

The attainment of these stars can dramatically impact a chef's career and a restaurant's success, leading to increased visibility, higher customer demand, and the ability to charge premium prices. The stars also serve as a benchmark for culinary excellence, influencing diners' choices and raising the standards across the industry.

Lee Hernandez's Journey to Michelin Stardom

Lee Hernandez's ascent to Michelin stardom began at his flagship restaurant, *Culinary Innovations*, where he introduced a unique blend of traditional techniques and modern food technology. His innovative approach to molecular gastronomy not only captivated diners but also impressed Michelin inspectors.

$$\text{Culinary Success} = f(\text{Innovation, Technique, Consistency}) \quad (60)$$

This equation illustrates that culinary success, as experienced by Hernandez, is a function of innovation in food preparation, mastery of cooking techniques, and consistency in delivering high-quality dishes. His signature dish, the *FlavorBurst™ Sphere*, exemplified this formula. This dish, which featured a delicate outer shell that burst with flavor upon consumption, was a testament to his culinary creativity and technical prowess.

Challenges in Achieving Michelin Recognition

However, the path to Michelin recognition is fraught with challenges. The competition is fierce, with numerous talented chefs vying for limited star allocations. Additionally, the Michelin Guide is known for its strict criteria and anonymous inspections, making it difficult for chefs to predict when and how they will be evaluated.

Lee faced skepticism from traditionalists who viewed his innovative techniques as gimmicks rather than legitimate culinary advancements. Overcoming this skepticism required not only exceptional culinary skills but also a commitment to educating the public and critics alike about the merits of food technology.

International Acclaim and Its Impact

Upon receiving his first Michelin star, Hernandez experienced a surge in international acclaim. Food critics and influencers began to take notice, leading to features in prestigious culinary publications and invitations to global food festivals. This newfound recognition allowed him to expand his culinary empire and explore new ventures, including collaborations with renowned chefs and participation in international culinary competitions.

The impact of Michelin recognition extends beyond personal accolades. It can elevate a city's culinary scene, attracting food enthusiasts and tourists alike. Cities with Michelin-starred restaurants often see increased economic benefits, including higher tourism rates and a boost to local businesses.

Conclusion

In conclusion, Michelin stars represent the pinnacle of culinary achievement, and for Lee Hernandez, they have been instrumental in establishing his reputation as a leading innovator in the food technology space. The challenges faced in achieving these accolades only serve to highlight the dedication and passion required to excel in this competitive industry. As Hernandez continues to push the boundaries of culinary innovation, his Michelin stars stand as a testament to his commitment to excellence and his influence on the global food landscape.

Induction into the Culinary Hall of Fame

Lee Hernandez's induction into the Culinary Hall of Fame marked a significant milestone not only in his career but also in the evolution of culinary arts as a whole. The Culinary Hall of Fame, established to honor individuals who have made extraordinary contributions to the culinary world, recognizes visionaries who have pushed the boundaries of gastronomy. Hernandez's innovative approach to food technology and his commitment to sustainability positioned him as a deserving candidate for this prestigious accolade.

Criteria for Induction

The selection process for the Culinary Hall of Fame is rigorous and multifaceted. Candidates are evaluated based on several criteria, including:

+ **Innovation:** The ability to introduce new techniques, flavors, or concepts that significantly impact the culinary landscape.

+ **Influence:** The extent to which a chef or food innovator has inspired others in the industry, including peers, students, and aspiring chefs.

+ **Sustainability:** Commitment to environmentally friendly practices and contributions towards reducing the ecological footprint of the food industry.

+ **Culinary Excellence:** Recognition through awards, accolades, and peer reviews that affirm the candidate's skill and artistry in the kitchen.

Hernandez's journey through these criteria exemplified his dedication to not only culinary excellence but also to the advancement of food technology.

Innovative Contributions

One of the primary reasons for Hernandez's induction was his groundbreaking work with FlavorBurst™, a product that revolutionized the way flavors are perceived and experienced. FlavorBurst™ utilized molecular gastronomy principles to enhance taste sensations without compromising nutritional value. This innovation addressed a significant problem in the culinary world: the challenge of creating flavorful yet healthy food options.

The equation governing the flavor enhancement process can be represented as:

$$F = \frac{C \cdot T}{D} \tag{61}$$

where:

+ F = Flavor intensity

+ C = Concentration of flavor compounds

+ T = Temperature at which the food is served

+ D = Density of the food medium

By manipulating these variables, Hernandez was able to create dishes that not only tantalized the taste buds but also catered to a health-conscious audience.

Impact on the Culinary Community

Hernandez's induction into the Hall of Fame served as an inspiration for many within the culinary community. His commitment to sustainability, particularly through initiatives aimed at reducing food waste, showcased a model that many chefs began to adopt. For instance, his collaboration with local farmers to source ingredients and minimize waste set a precedent in the industry.

Moreover, Hernandez's mentorship of young chefs has led to the emergence of a new generation of culinary innovators. His workshops and seminars on food technology have empowered aspiring chefs to explore the intersection of science and culinary arts. As a testament to his influence, many of his mentees have gone on to achieve significant recognition themselves, further solidifying Hernandez's legacy.

Recognition and Awards

The culmination of Hernandez's achievements was celebrated during the induction ceremony, where he was honored alongside other culinary luminaries. The ceremony highlighted not only his individual accomplishments but also the collective progress within the culinary arts, particularly in the realm of food technology.

Hernandez's acceptance speech resonated with attendees, as he emphasized the importance of innovation in addressing global challenges such as food insecurity and climate change. He stated, "We have a responsibility not just to create delicious food, but to ensure that our innovations contribute positively to the world around us."

Conclusion

In conclusion, Lee Hernandez's induction into the Culinary Hall of Fame is a testament to his visionary approach to food technology and his unwavering commitment to culinary excellence. His innovations, particularly with FlavorBurst™, have not only transformed the dining experience but have also inspired a new wave of culinary thinkers dedicated to sustainability and creativity. As Hernandez continues to mentor the next generation of chefs, his legacy will undoubtedly shape the future of the culinary world for years to come.

Philanthropy and giving back

Establishing scholarships for aspiring chefs

In the culinary world, the journey to becoming a successful chef is often fraught with challenges, particularly for those from underprivileged backgrounds. Establishing scholarships for aspiring chefs serves as a crucial step toward democratizing access to culinary education and empowering the next generation of culinary innovators. These scholarships not only alleviate the financial burden of culinary school tuition but also provide mentorship and resources that can significantly enhance a student's educational experience.

The Importance of Scholarships

The culinary industry is known for its high costs associated with formal education. According to the National Center for Education Statistics, the average cost of attending a culinary school can range from $20,000 to $50,000 per year. This financial barrier disproportionately affects aspiring chefs from low-income families, who may lack the necessary resources to pursue their dreams. Scholarships can bridge this gap, enabling talented individuals to access quality education and training without the crippling weight of student debt.

Moreover, scholarships can foster diversity within the culinary field. By targeting underrepresented groups, these programs can help cultivate a more inclusive environment that reflects the rich tapestry of cultures and cuisines around the world. As Lee Hernandez has demonstrated through his initiatives, investing in diverse culinary talent not only enriches the industry but also leads to innovative culinary creations that resonate with a broader audience.

Challenges Faced by Aspiring Chefs

Despite the availability of scholarships, many aspiring chefs still encounter significant hurdles. The competitive nature of culinary programs means that even those who excel academically may struggle to secure funding. Additionally, the lack of awareness about available scholarships can prevent talented individuals from applying.

Furthermore, the culinary field often demands long hours and intense physical labor, which can deter potential applicants who may not see a clear path to a sustainable career. This is where scholarships can play a transformative role by providing not just financial support, but also career guidance and networking opportunities that can lead to internships and job placements.

Successful Scholarship Programs

Several successful scholarship programs exemplify the positive impact of financial support in the culinary arts. For instance, the James Beard Foundation offers a scholarship program that awards thousands of dollars to students pursuing culinary arts, food studies, and related fields. The program emphasizes diversity and aims to support individuals who demonstrate a commitment to the culinary profession.

Another notable example is the Culinary Institute of America's (CIA) scholarship program, which provides financial assistance to students based on merit and need. The CIA has established partnerships with various organizations to fund scholarships specifically for minorities and women, thereby promoting inclusivity within the culinary landscape.

Conclusion

In conclusion, establishing scholarships for aspiring chefs is a vital investment in the future of the culinary arts. By removing financial barriers and fostering diversity, these scholarships can help cultivate a new generation of culinary innovators who are equipped to tackle the challenges of the modern food industry. As Lee Hernandez continues to champion the cause of aspiring chefs, his efforts in establishing scholarships will undoubtedly leave a lasting legacy that inspires countless individuals to pursue their culinary dreams.

$$\text{Access to Education} = \text{Financial Support} + \text{Mentorship} + \text{Networking Opportunities} \tag{62}$$

This equation highlights the multifaceted approach needed to ensure that aspiring chefs not only gain access to culinary education but also thrive in their careers.

Supporting sustainable food initiatives

In an era where environmental concerns are at the forefront of global discourse, Lee Hernandez has emerged as a pivotal figure in promoting sustainable food practices. His commitment to sustainability is not merely a peripheral aspect of his culinary empire; it is an integral part of his philosophy and business model. This section delves into the various sustainable food initiatives that Hernandez has supported, illustrating how they contribute to a healthier planet and society.

Understanding Sustainable Food Systems

Sustainable food systems are defined as those that provide food security and nutrition for all while minimizing environmental impacts, promoting social equity, and enhancing economic viability. According to the Food and Agriculture Organization (FAO), sustainable food production must be able to feed a growing population without compromising the ability of future generations to meet their own needs [?]. This approach encompasses several key principles:

- **Environmental Stewardship:** Practices that conserve biodiversity, reduce pollution, and enhance ecosystem resilience.

- **Social Responsibility:** Ensuring fair labor practices, supporting local communities, and promoting health and well-being.

- **Economic Viability:** Creating systems that are economically sustainable for farmers, producers, and consumers alike.

Hernandez's initiatives align closely with these principles, showcasing how culinary innovation can lead to sustainable practices.

Innovative Partnerships with Local Farmers

One of the cornerstone initiatives of Hernandez's approach to sustainability is his collaboration with local farmers. By sourcing ingredients from nearby farms, he reduces the carbon footprint associated with transportation and supports the local economy. This practice is rooted in the concept of *food miles*, which refers to the distance food travels from production to consumption. The equation for calculating food miles can be expressed as:

$$\text{Food Miles} = \sum_{i=1}^{n} d_i \cdot q_i$$

where d_i is the distance from the farm to the consumer and q_i is the quantity of food produced by that farm. By minimizing food miles, Hernandez not only promotes fresher ingredients but also contributes to reduced greenhouse gas emissions.

Waste Reduction Strategies

Another significant aspect of Hernandez's commitment to sustainability is his focus on reducing food waste. According to the United Nations, approximately one-third of all food produced globally is wasted, contributing to environmental degradation and food insecurity [?]. Hernandez has implemented several strategies to combat this issue:

- **Upcycling Ingredients:** Transforming food scraps and by-products into new culinary creations. For instance, vegetable peels can be turned into chips or broths, thereby minimizing waste.

- **Composting Programs:** Establishing composting systems within his restaurants to recycle organic waste, which can then be used to enrich soil for local farms.

- **Educating Consumers:** Hosting workshops to raise awareness about the importance of reducing food waste at home, encouraging consumers to utilize leftovers creatively.

These initiatives not only help in reducing waste but also foster a culture of sustainability among consumers.

Advocacy for Plant-Based Diets

Recognizing the significant environmental impact of animal agriculture, Hernandez has been a vocal advocate for plant-based diets. Research indicates that shifting towards a more plant-based diet can lead to substantial reductions in greenhouse gas emissions, land use, and water consumption [?]. Hernandez has integrated this philosophy into his culinary offerings by:

- **Developing Plant-Based Products:** Creating innovative plant-based alternatives that appeal to both vegans and non-vegans alike. His flagship product, FlavorBurst™, includes a range of plant-based flavor enhancers that elevate the taste of dishes without relying on animal products.

- **Promoting Seasonal Eating:** Encouraging consumers to eat seasonally by featuring dishes that highlight local, in-season produce. This practice not only supports local farmers but also reduces the environmental impact associated with out-of-season produce.

Community Engagement and Education

Hernandez understands that lasting change requires community involvement and education. He has initiated several programs aimed at educating the public about sustainable food practices:

- **Workshops and Seminars:** Hosting events focused on sustainable cooking techniques, nutrition, and the importance of supporting local agriculture.

- **School Programs:** Partnering with local schools to introduce students to gardening and cooking, fostering an appreciation for fresh, sustainable food from a young age.

- **Social Media Campaigns:** Utilizing his platform to raise awareness about sustainability issues, share recipes, and promote local food initiatives.

These efforts not only empower individuals to make informed food choices but also cultivate a community dedicated to sustainability.

Conclusion

Lee Hernandez's support for sustainable food initiatives exemplifies how culinary innovation can drive positive change in the food industry. By fostering partnerships with local farmers, implementing waste reduction strategies, advocating for plant-based diets, and engaging with the community, Hernandez is not only transforming the culinary landscape but also contributing to a more sustainable future.   His work serves as an inspiration for aspiring food entrepreneurs, demonstrating that it is possible to blend passion for food with a commitment to environmental stewardship.

Using fame to advocate for a better food system

In recent years, the intersection of celebrity culture and social advocacy has become increasingly prominent, particularly in the realm of food systems. Lee Hernandez, with his meteoric rise in the culinary world, has harnessed his fame not only to elevate his brand but also to champion significant changes in food production, accessibility, and sustainability. This section explores how Hernandez uses his platform to advocate for a better food system, addressing both the theoretical frameworks and practical implications of his efforts.

Theoretical Framework

The advocacy for a better food system can be understood through various theoretical lenses. One such framework is the **Social Change Theory**, which posits that individuals with high visibility can influence public opinion and drive societal change. Hernandez exemplifies this theory as he leverages his celebrity status to bring attention to pressing issues within the food industry, such as food waste, sustainable practices, and equitable access to nutritious food.

Moreover, the **Sustainable Development Goals (SDGs)** set forth by the United Nations provide a guiding framework for Hernandez's advocacy. Specifically, Goal 2 emphasizes the need for zero hunger, promoting sustainable agriculture, and ensuring food security. By aligning his initiatives with these global goals, Hernandez not only enhances his credibility but also mobilizes a broader audience towards collective action.

Identifying Problems

Despite the advancements in food technology and culinary innovation, several systemic issues persist within the food system. These include:

- **Food Insecurity:** Millions of people globally face hunger and malnutrition. According to the Food and Agriculture Organization (FAO), approximately

690 million people were undernourished in 2019, a number exacerbated by the COVID-19 pandemic.

+ **Food Waste:** The United Nations estimates that one-third of all food produced for human consumption is wasted each year, amounting to 1.3 billion tons. This waste not only represents a loss of resources but also contributes to greenhouse gas emissions.

+ **Unsustainable Practices:** Conventional farming practices often lead to soil degradation, loss of biodiversity, and over-reliance on chemical inputs, which can harm both the environment and human health.

Hernandez's advocacy seeks to address these challenges by promoting innovative solutions that can transform the food landscape.

Practical Initiatives

Hernandez's commitment to advocacy is evident through various initiatives and partnerships aimed at reforming the food system:

1. **Public Awareness Campaigns:** Utilizing social media and public appearances, Hernandez raises awareness about food waste and encourages consumers to adopt more sustainable practices. For instance, his campaign, *Waste Not, Want Not,* encourages restaurants and households to rethink their food disposal habits, highlighting the environmental impact of waste.

2. **Collaborations with Nonprofits:** Partnering with organizations like *Feeding America,* Hernandez has worked to combat food insecurity by donating a portion of his profits to provide meals for those in need. His involvement not only provides financial support but also brings visibility to the issue, inspiring others in the industry to contribute.

3. **Sustainable Product Development:** Through his company, Culinary Innovations Inc., Hernandez has developed products that prioritize sustainability, such as plant-based alternatives and upcycled ingredients. By creating demand for these products, he helps shift consumer behavior towards more sustainable choices.

4. **Educational Programs:** Hernandez has established culinary scholarships and training programs aimed at underserved communities, fostering the next generation of food innovators. By investing in education, he ensures

that diverse voices are represented in the culinary field, leading to a more inclusive food system.

Case Studies and Examples

Several notable examples illustrate how Hernandez has successfully utilized his fame to advocate for a better food system:

- **FlavorBurst™ and Food Waste Reduction:** The launch of his FlavorBurst™ product line not only introduced innovative flavor profiles but also emphasized the use of ingredients that would otherwise go to waste. This initiative garnered attention from both consumers and industry leaders, showcasing how culinary innovation can align with sustainability.

- **Media Appearances and Advocacy:** In various interviews and cooking shows, Hernandez has consistently highlighted the importance of sustainable practices. His participation in documentaries focused on food systems has educated viewers on the intricacies of food production and the necessity for reform.

- **Social Media Influence:** With millions of followers across platforms, Hernandez uses his social media presence to share recipes, tips for reducing food waste, and information on sustainable farming practices. His engaging content not only entertains but also educates his audience, fostering a community of informed consumers.

Conclusion

Lee Hernandez's journey as a culinary innovator transcends the kitchen; it embodies a commitment to advocating for a better food system. By leveraging his fame, he addresses critical issues such as food insecurity, waste, and unsustainable practices, fostering a movement towards a more equitable and sustainable food landscape. As he continues to inspire others through his initiatives, Hernandez exemplifies the potential of celebrity advocacy to effect meaningful change in the food industry and beyond.

Legacy and Future Outlook

Cementing a lasting legacy

Securing the future of Culinary Innovations Inc.

In the rapidly evolving landscape of food technology, securing the future of *Culinary Innovations Inc.* (CII) requires a multifaceted approach that integrates sustainability, innovation, and market adaptability. As Lee Hernandez navigates the complexities of the food industry, several key strategies emerge to ensure the longevity and impact of his company.

Sustainability as a Core Principle

One of the foremost strategies for securing the future of CII is embedding sustainability into the core of its operations. The food industry faces significant challenges, including climate change, resource depletion, and food waste. According to the Food and Agriculture Organization (FAO), approximately one-third of all food produced globally is wasted, which equates to about 1.3 billion tons annually [?].

To combat this, CII has adopted a **sustainable sourcing policy** that prioritizes local and organic ingredients. This approach not only reduces carbon footprints associated with transportation but also supports local economies. For example, by partnering with local farmers, CII can ensure that its products are fresh while also fostering community relationships.

Innovative Product Development

Innovation is at the heart of CII's strategy. The company continuously invests in research and development to create new products that meet emerging consumer demands. One notable example is the development of *FlavorBurst™*, a product that utilizes advanced food technology to enhance flavor profiles without the use of artificial additives. This innovation aligns with the growing consumer preference for clean label products, which emphasize transparency and healthfulness.

The theory of disruptive innovation [?] can be applied here, as CII aims to disrupt traditional food manufacturing processes by introducing novel techniques such as molecular gastronomy and 3D food printing. These technologies allow for the creation of unique culinary experiences that can attract a diverse customer base, from gourmet restaurants to everyday consumers.

Market Adaptability

The food industry is characterized by rapid shifts in consumer preferences and market trends. To secure its future, CII must remain adaptable and responsive to these changes. This involves not only monitoring market trends but also engaging with consumers directly to gather feedback and insights.

For instance, the rise of plant-based diets has prompted CII to expand its product line to include plant-based alternatives that cater to this demographic. According to a report by the Plant Based Foods Association, the plant-based food market grew by 27% in 2020, indicating a significant shift in consumer behavior [?]. By aligning product offerings with consumer trends, CII positions itself as a leader in the food technology space.

Strategic Partnerships and Collaborations

Another critical aspect of securing the future of CII is forming strategic partnerships and collaborations. By collaborating with research institutions, universities, and other food tech companies, CII can leverage shared knowledge and resources to accelerate innovation. For example, partnerships with universities can facilitate access to cutting-edge research in food science, enabling CII to stay ahead of industry trends.

Additionally, collaborations with sustainability-focused organizations can enhance CII's reputation and credibility in the market. By participating in initiatives aimed at reducing food waste or promoting sustainable agriculture, CII not only contributes to broader societal goals but also builds brand loyalty among environmentally conscious consumers.

Investment in Technology

Investing in technology is essential for the future of CII. The integration of artificial intelligence (AI) and data analytics into food production processes can lead to increased efficiency and reduced waste. For instance, AI algorithms can predict consumer demand patterns, allowing CII to optimize production schedules and minimize excess inventory.

The equation for calculating the optimal production quantity can be expressed as follows:

$$Q^* = \sqrt{\frac{2DS}{H}} \tag{63}$$

Where:

+ Q^* = Optimal order quantity

+ D = Demand rate (units/year)

+ S = Setup cost per order

+ H = Holding cost per unit per year

By applying this formula, CII can streamline its operations, reduce costs, and improve overall profitability.

Engaging with the Community

Lastly, engaging with the community is vital for securing the future of Culinary Innovations Inc. By fostering relationships with customers, CII can build a loyal consumer base that advocates for its products. Community engagement initiatives, such as cooking classes, food festivals, and educational workshops, can enhance brand visibility and create a sense of belonging among consumers.

Moreover, CII's commitment to philanthropy, such as supporting local food banks and culinary scholarships, reinforces its dedication to social responsibility. This not only enhances the company's image but also ensures that it remains relevant in an increasingly socially conscious market.

In conclusion, securing the future of Culinary Innovations Inc. involves a comprehensive strategy that prioritizes sustainability, innovation, market adaptability, strategic partnerships, technology investment, and community engagement. By embracing these principles, Lee Hernandez can ensure that CII not only thrives in the competitive food technology landscape but also leaves a lasting positive impact on the industry and society as a whole.

Mentoring the next generation of food innovators

In the rapidly evolving landscape of food technology, the importance of mentorship cannot be overstated. Lee Hernandez, recognizing the need for guidance and support in the culinary field, has dedicated a significant portion of his career to mentoring aspiring food innovators. This commitment stems from his belief that the future of food lies not only in technological advancements but also in the nurturing of young talent who will drive these innovations forward.

The Role of Mentorship

Mentorship plays a crucial role in shaping the careers of young chefs and food technologists. According to a study published in the *Journal of Culinary Science and Technology*, mentorship enhances professional development by providing mentees with valuable insights, networking opportunities, and emotional support [?]. The relationship between a mentor and mentee can be likened to the process of fermentation in cooking; it requires time, patience, and the right conditions to yield the best results.

Lee's approach to mentorship is multifaceted. He emphasizes the importance of both technical skills and creative thinking, encouraging his mentees to experiment and push the boundaries of traditional culinary practices. As he often states, "Innovation in food requires a willingness to fail, learn, and try again." This philosophy is crucial in an industry where the stakes are high, and the pressure to deliver exceptional results can be overwhelming.

Challenges Faced by Aspiring Innovators

Despite the promising future of food technology, aspiring innovators face numerous challenges. One of the most significant issues is the lack of access to resources and funding. Many talented individuals come from backgrounds where culinary education is not financially feasible, leading to a talent drain in the industry. According to the *National Restaurant Association*, nearly 60% of culinary students cite financial constraints as a barrier to their education [?].

Additionally, the fast-paced nature of the food industry can be intimidating for newcomers. The pressure to keep up with trends, consumer demands, and technological advancements can lead to burnout. Lee addresses these challenges by creating a supportive environment where mentees can express their concerns and seek advice. He believes that a strong mentor-mentee relationship can help alleviate some of the stress associated with entering such a competitive field.

Practical Examples of Mentorship in Action

One of the most notable examples of Lee's mentorship is his work with the *Culinary Futures Program*, an initiative designed to provide young chefs with the tools and knowledge necessary to succeed in the food technology sector. The program includes workshops, hands-on training, and opportunities to collaborate with industry leaders. Participants are encouraged to develop their own innovative food products, fostering a sense of ownership and creativity.

A standout success story from the program is that of Jamie Lin, a young chef who developed a plant-based alternative to traditional dairy products. Under Lee's guidance, Jamie navigated the complexities of food science, experimenting with various ingredients and techniques to create a product that not only met consumer demands for sustainability but also appealed to the palate. Jamie's product, *CreamyGreen*, has since gained traction in the market, showcasing the potential of mentorship to spark innovation.

The Impact of Mentorship on the Industry

Lee's commitment to mentoring has far-reaching implications for the culinary world. By investing in the next generation of food innovators, he is not only ensuring the continuation of culinary excellence but also fostering a culture of collaboration and creativity. This is particularly important in an era where the food industry faces pressing challenges such as climate change, food security, and health concerns.

As aspiring chefs and food technologists emerge from mentorship programs equipped with the skills and confidence to innovate, they contribute to a more sustainable and equitable food system. This ripple effect can be seen in the growing trend of young entrepreneurs launching their own food tech startups, often with a focus on sustainability and social responsibility.

In conclusion, Lee Hernandez's dedication to mentoring the next generation of food innovators is a testament to his belief in the power of collaboration and creativity. By nurturing young talent, he is not only shaping the future of food technology but also leaving a lasting legacy that will inspire future generations to pursue their culinary dreams. As the industry continues to evolve, the importance of mentorship will remain a cornerstone of innovation, ensuring that the future of food is bright and full of possibilities.

Preservation and expansion of flavor profiles

The preservation and expansion of flavor profiles is a critical aspect of culinary innovation that aims to enhance the sensory experience of food while maintaining its integrity and sustainability. In the context of Lee Hernandez's contributions to food technology, this section explores the theoretical underpinnings, challenges, and practical examples of how flavor profiles can be preserved and expanded.

Theoretical Framework

Flavor is a complex interplay of taste, aroma, and mouthfeel, which can be quantified and analyzed through various scientific methods. The primary tastes recognized are sweet, sour, salty, bitter, and umami, while aroma compounds, which can number in the thousands, significantly contribute to the overall flavor experience. The following equation represents the interaction of these components:

$$F = f(T, A, M) \tag{64}$$

where F is the overall flavor profile, T represents taste components, A denotes aroma compounds, and M signifies mouthfeel attributes. This equation underscores the need for a holistic approach to flavor development, emphasizing that each component must be carefully balanced.

Challenges in Flavor Preservation

Preserving flavor profiles poses several challenges, particularly in the face of modern food production methods. Factors such as temperature fluctuations, exposure to light, and oxygen can lead to the degradation of flavor compounds. For instance, the Maillard reaction, a crucial process in developing flavor in cooked foods, can be adversely affected by improper storage conditions. Additionally, the use of preservatives and artificial flavor enhancers can alter the natural flavor profiles, leading to a loss of authenticity.

To combat these challenges, food technologists employ various preservation techniques, including:

- **Vacuum sealing:** This method reduces oxygen exposure, thus slowing down the oxidation of flavor compounds.

- **Fermentation:** Utilizing beneficial bacteria and yeasts can enhance and preserve flavor while introducing new taste dimensions.

- **Cold storage:** Maintaining low temperatures can help retain the integrity of volatile aroma compounds.

Expanding Flavor Profiles

In addition to preservation, expanding flavor profiles involves innovation and creativity in flavor development. This process can be driven by several factors, including consumer preferences, cultural influences, and advancements in food technology. Techniques such as molecular gastronomy allow chefs to manipulate flavor components at a molecular level, creating new and exciting flavor combinations.

One notable example of flavor expansion is the use of flavor pairing, which is based on the principle that ingredients sharing similar aroma compounds can create harmonious dishes. Research conducted by food scientists has shown that certain flavor compounds can be combined to produce unique and unexpected flavor experiences. For instance, the pairing of chocolate with blue cheese has gained popularity due to their shared aromatic compounds, leading to a complex and rich flavor profile.

Moreover, the incorporation of global flavors into traditional dishes has become a hallmark of contemporary cuisine. Lee Hernandez's culinary innovations often explore the fusion of disparate culinary traditions, resulting in dishes that surprise and delight the palate. An example of this is his creation of a spicy mango salsa that incorporates traditional Mexican flavors with Asian-inspired ingredients like ginger and sesame.

Conclusion

The preservation and expansion of flavor profiles are vital to the future of culinary innovation. Through a combination of scientific understanding and creative exploration, food technologists like Lee Hernandez are redefining what is possible in the culinary world. By addressing the challenges of flavor preservation and embracing the potential for flavor expansion, the food industry can continue to evolve, offering consumers new and exciting taste experiences while honoring the rich traditions of global cuisine.

In summary, the careful balance between preserving the essence of flavors and expanding upon them is a testament to the artistry and science of modern cooking. As we look to the future, the potential for innovative flavor profiles remains limitless, driven by the passion of culinary innovators dedicated to pushing the boundaries of what food can be.

The future of food technology

Predictions and possibilities

The future of food technology is poised to undergo transformative changes, driven by advancements in science, technology, and changing consumer preferences. As we look ahead, several key predictions can be made regarding the evolution of food technology, each with its own set of possibilities and challenges.

Personalized Nutrition

One of the most significant trends in food technology is the move towards personalized nutrition. Advances in genomics and biotechnology allow us to tailor diets to individual genetic profiles, health needs, and lifestyle choices. This concept, often referred to as nutrigenomics, suggests that food can be customized to enhance health and prevent diseases.

$$Nutritional\ Value = f(Genetic\ Profile, Lifestyle\ Factors, Health\ Conditic$$
$$(65)$$

Where: - $Nutritional\ Value$ is the tailored dietary recommendation. - f represents a function that correlates genetic and lifestyle data with optimal nutrition.

For example, individuals with a genetic predisposition to lactose intolerance can receive personalized recommendations for lactose-free alternatives, while those with a family history of heart disease might be advised to increase their omega-3 fatty acid intake. However, this raises ethical questions about privacy, data security, and the accessibility of such personalized solutions.

Sustainable Food Production

Sustainability is no longer just a trend; it is a necessity. The food industry is expected to embrace innovative practices that minimize environmental impact. Techniques such as vertical farming, aquaponics, and lab-grown meats are gaining traction as solutions to the challenges of food security and environmental degradation.

$$Environmental\ Impact = \frac{Total\ Emissions}{Food\ Production\ Volume} \quad (66)$$

Where: - $Total\ Emissions$ refers to greenhouse gases released during production. - $Food\ Production\ Volume$ is the total amount of food produced.

For instance, vertical farms utilize significantly less land and water compared to traditional farming, while also reducing transportation emissions by being located in urban areas. Furthermore, lab-grown meat has the potential to drastically cut down on methane emissions associated with livestock farming. Nevertheless, achieving widespread adoption of these technologies will require overcoming regulatory hurdles and consumer acceptance.

The Role of Artificial Intelligence

Artificial intelligence (AI) is set to revolutionize the food industry by optimizing supply chains, enhancing food safety, and improving customer experiences. AI algorithms can analyze vast amounts of data to predict consumer preferences, streamline production processes, and reduce waste.

$$Efficiency = \frac{Output}{Input} \tag{67}$$

Where: - $Output$ is the total amount of food produced or sold. - $Input$ is the resources utilized (e.g., time, labor, materials).

For example, grocery stores are increasingly using AI to manage inventory and reduce food spoilage. By predicting demand patterns, they can adjust orders accordingly, minimizing waste and maximizing profits. However, the reliance on AI also raises concerns about job displacement and the need for human oversight in decision-making processes.

Global Food Security

As the global population continues to grow, ensuring food security will be paramount. Innovations in food technology will play a crucial role in addressing hunger and malnutrition, particularly in developing countries. Technologies such as biofortification, which enhances the nutritional quality of staple crops, and mobile applications that provide farmers with real-time information on weather and market prices are vital tools in this effort.

$$Food\ Security = \frac{Access\ to\ Nutrition}{Population\ Growth} \tag{68}$$

Where: - $Access\ to\ Nutrition$ represents the availability and affordability of food. - $Population\ Growth$ is the increase in the number of people requiring sustenance.

For instance, the introduction of drought-resistant crops can significantly improve food availability in regions prone to climate change. However, ensuring equitable access to these technologies remains a challenge, particularly for smallholder farmers.

Ethical and Cultural Considerations

As food technology evolves, ethical considerations surrounding biotechnology, animal welfare, and cultural food practices will become increasingly prominent. The acceptance of genetically modified organisms (GMOs) and lab-grown foods varies widely across cultures, and addressing these concerns will be crucial for the successful integration of new technologies.

$$Cultural\ Acceptance = f(Tradition, Education, Awareness) \qquad (69)$$

Where: - *Cultural Acceptance* is the degree to which a society embraces new food technologies. - *Tradition* refers to established food practices. - *Education* and *Awareness* denote the knowledge and understanding of new technologies.

For example, while some cultures may embrace plant-based alternatives as a sustainable solution, others may resist due to traditional dietary practices. Engaging communities in discussions about the benefits and risks of food technology will be essential for fostering acceptance and ensuring that innovations align with cultural values.

Conclusion

In conclusion, the future of food technology is ripe with potential, offering solutions to some of the most pressing challenges faced by our global food system. By harnessing the power of personalized nutrition, sustainable practices, artificial intelligence, and innovative approaches to food security, we can create a more equitable and efficient food landscape. However, navigating the ethical and cultural implications of these advancements will be key to their successful implementation. As we move forward, it is crucial to remain vigilant and proactive in addressing the complexities that arise, ensuring that the innovations of tomorrow contribute positively to society as a whole.

The role of food tech in addressing global challenges

The intersection of food technology and global challenges presents a unique opportunity for innovation and sustainable development. As the world grapples with issues such as climate change, food insecurity, and health crises, food tech emerges as a pivotal player in crafting solutions that can mitigate these pressing problems.

Food Security and Accessibility

Food security is defined as the condition in which all people have physical, social, and economic access to sufficient, safe, and nutritious food to meet their dietary needs and food preferences for an active and healthy life. According to the Food and Agriculture Organization (FAO), approximately 690 million people are undernourished globally, a figure that has been exacerbated by the COVID-19 pandemic. Food tech can address these challenges through innovative approaches such as vertical farming, which maximizes space and resource efficiency.

$$\text{Yield}_{\text{vertical}} = \frac{\text{Total Area} \times \text{Crop Density}}{\text{Growth Cycle}} \tag{70}$$

This equation highlights that by increasing crop density and optimizing growth cycles, vertical farms can produce significantly more food per square foot compared to traditional farming. For instance, companies like AeroFarms and Plenty have successfully implemented vertical farming systems that yield up to 390 times more produce per square foot annually than conventional farms.

Sustainability and Environmental Impact

The agricultural sector is a major contributor to greenhouse gas emissions, accounting for approximately 24% of total emissions. Food tech innovations such as precision agriculture, which utilizes data analytics and IoT (Internet of Things) technologies, can significantly reduce the environmental footprint of food production.

$$\text{Emissions Reduction} = \text{Baseline Emissions} - \text{Post-Tech Emissions} \tag{71}$$

By employing sensors to monitor soil health, moisture levels, and crop growth, farmers can optimize resource usage, thereby reducing waste and emissions. For example, the use of drones for crop monitoring has allowed farmers to apply fertilizers and pesticides more efficiently, resulting in reduced chemical runoff into waterways and lower overall emissions.

Health and Nutrition

Food technology also plays a crucial role in addressing public health challenges related to diet and nutrition. The rise of non-communicable diseases (NCDs) such as obesity and diabetes has prompted a shift towards healthier food options. Innovations in food tech, such as the development of plant-based proteins and alternative meat products, provide consumers with healthier choices that can also reduce the environmental impact of meat production.

For example, companies like Beyond Meat and Impossible Foods have created plant-based alternatives that closely mimic the taste and texture of beef, appealing to both vegetarians and meat-eaters alike. These products not only cater to dietary preferences but also contribute to a decrease in livestock farming, which is a significant source of methane emissions.

Waste Reduction and Circular Economy

Food waste is another critical issue, with approximately one-third of all food produced globally being wasted. Food tech innovations such as smart packaging and food preservation technologies can help extend the shelf life of products and reduce waste. The concept of a circular economy in food production emphasizes the importance of reusing and recycling food resources.

$$\text{Waste Reduction} = \text{Initial Waste} - \text{Recycled/Repurposed Waste} \qquad (72)$$

For instance, companies are now developing biodegradable packaging that can decompose more quickly than traditional plastics, thereby minimizing landfill contributions. Additionally, initiatives that convert food waste into energy or compost can significantly reduce the environmental impact of discarded food.

Conclusion

In conclusion, food technology stands at the forefront of addressing global challenges such as food security, sustainability, health, and waste reduction. By leveraging innovative solutions, food tech not only enhances food production efficiency but also promotes a healthier and more sustainable food system. As Lee Hernandez continues to pioneer advancements in this field, the potential for food tech to create lasting positive change in the world remains immense. The future of food is not only about nourishment but also about creating a resilient and equitable food system for generations to come.

Lee Hernandez's enduring impact on the industry

Lee Hernandez's influence on the culinary landscape extends far beyond his innovative products and entrepreneurial success. His work has not only transformed the way food is prepared and consumed but has also laid the groundwork for future advancements in food technology. This section will explore the multifaceted impact of Hernandez's contributions, highlighting key theories, problems addressed, and notable examples that illustrate his enduring legacy in the food industry.

Redefining Culinary Boundaries

Hernandez's pioneering approach to food technology has redefined traditional culinary boundaries. By integrating scientific principles with culinary arts, he has introduced concepts such as molecular gastronomy into mainstream cooking. This fusion of disciplines challenges the notion of cooking as merely an art form, positioning it as a science that can be studied, measured, and innovated upon.

For instance, the equation for the Maillard reaction, a fundamental chemical reaction in cooking, can be expressed as:

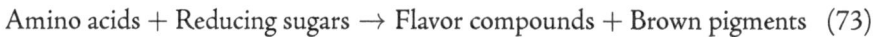

$$\text{Amino acids} + \text{Reducing sugars} \rightarrow \text{Flavor compounds} + \text{Brown pigments} \quad (73)$$

Hernandez's emphasis on understanding such reactions has led to the development of new cooking techniques that enhance flavor profiles and textures, allowing chefs to create dishes that were previously unimaginable.

Addressing Food Sustainability

One of the most pressing challenges facing the global food industry today is sustainability. Hernandez has been at the forefront of initiatives aimed at reducing food waste and promoting sustainable practices. His collaboration with farmers and suppliers has led to innovative solutions that not only minimize waste but also enhance the quality of food produced.

For example, his company, Culinary Innovations Inc., implemented a system known as "Farm-to-Fork Optimization," which utilizes data analytics to streamline the supply chain. The optimization can be modeled as follows:

$$\text{Efficiency} = \frac{\text{Total Output}}{\text{Total Input}} \quad (74)$$

This approach has resulted in a significant reduction in food waste, demonstrating that sustainable practices can be both economically viable and environmentally responsible.

Inspiring a New Generation

Hernandez's impact is also evident in his role as a mentor and educator. By establishing scholarships and programs for aspiring chefs, he has fostered a new generation of culinary innovators who are equipped with the skills and knowledge to continue pushing the boundaries of food technology. His mentorship emphasizes the importance of creativity and scientific inquiry, encouraging young chefs to experiment and explore new ideas.

The theory of creative problem-solving, which can be described using the following model, is central to Hernandez's mentorship approach:

$$\text{Problem Identification} \rightarrow \text{Idea Generation} \rightarrow \text{Prototype Development} \rightarrow \text{Testing and} \tag{75}$$

This iterative process not only cultivates innovation but also instills a sense of resilience in young chefs, preparing them to face the challenges of the culinary industry.

Global Influence and Cultural Fusion

Hernandez's work has also had a significant impact on global food culture. By championing fusion cuisine, he has encouraged the blending of culinary traditions from around the world, promoting diversity and inclusivity within the food industry. His signature dishes often incorporate elements from various cuisines, showcasing the potential for collaboration and creativity.

An example of this cultural fusion can be seen in his creation of the "Sushi Taco," which combines traditional Japanese sushi ingredients with the handheld convenience of a Mexican taco. This dish not only reflects the globalized nature of contemporary cuisine but also serves as a testament to Hernandez's belief in the power of culinary innovation to bridge cultural divides.

Lasting Innovations

The innovations introduced by Hernandez have had a lasting impact on the food industry, particularly in the realm of food technology. His development of FlavorBurst™, a product that enhances taste without the need for artificial additives, has set a new standard for flavor enhancement in food products. The underlying technology utilizes encapsulation techniques that can be described mathematically as:

$$\text{Flavor Release} = \text{Concentration} \times \text{Surface Area} \times \text{Diffusion Coefficient} \quad (76)$$

This innovation not only addresses consumer demand for healthier options but also inspires further research into natural flavor enhancement methods.

Conclusion: An Enduring Legacy

In conclusion, Lee Hernandez's enduring impact on the culinary industry is characterized by his innovative spirit, commitment to sustainability, and dedication to mentorship. His work has redefined culinary practices, inspired a new generation of chefs, and addressed critical challenges facing the food industry today. As we look to the future of food technology, Hernandez's legacy will undoubtedly continue to influence and shape the culinary landscape for years to come.

Conclusion: Lee Hernandez's Culinary Journey

Reflections on a remarkable career

Lessons learned along the way

Lee Hernandez's culinary journey has been a rich tapestry of experiences, challenges, and triumphs, each contributing to the lessons that have shaped his approach to food technology and innovation. These lessons extend beyond the kitchen, resonating with anyone seeking to carve their path in a competitive and ever-evolving landscape.

Embracing Failure as a Stepping Stone

One of the most profound lessons Lee learned was the importance of embracing failure. In the culinary world, not every experiment yields a successful dish. During his early years at the Institute of Culinary Arts, Lee faced numerous setbacks, particularly when experimenting with molecular gastronomy. For instance, one of his initial attempts to create a flavor-infused foam resulted in a texture that was more akin to a soggy sponge than a culinary delight.

This experience taught Lee that failure is not the end but rather a crucial part of the learning process. As he often says, "Each flop is a flavor waiting to be discovered." By analyzing what went wrong and adjusting his techniques, he was able to refine his approach and eventually create the revolutionary FlavorBurst™ product. This philosophy aligns with the scientific method, where hypotheses are tested, and failures lead to new insights and improvements.

The Value of Collaboration

Another significant lesson for Lee was the value of collaboration. His apprenticeship at Xperimental Foods Inc. exposed him to a diverse group of scientists and chefs, each bringing unique perspectives to the table. One memorable project involved working with a food scientist to develop a new preservation technique that utilized natural enzymes to extend the shelf life of fresh produce without compromising flavor.

Through collaboration, Lee learned that innovation often stems from the intersection of different disciplines. The blending of culinary arts with food science not only expanded his knowledge but also led to groundbreaking discoveries. This experience reinforced the idea that teamwork fosters creativity and problem-solving, essential components in the fast-paced food technology sector.

Balancing Tradition with Innovation

While Lee was passionate about pushing culinary boundaries, he also recognized the importance of honoring tradition. Growing up in a food-centric family, he was deeply influenced by his grandmother's recipes, which were steeped in cultural significance. As he ventured into food technology, he faced the challenge of integrating traditional flavors with modern techniques.

For example, when developing his plant-based product line, Lee sought to replicate the umami flavor found in traditional meat dishes. By utilizing fermentation—a technique rooted in culinary history—he was able to create a plant-based burger that satisfied both flavor and texture, earning accolades from both traditionalists and innovators alike. This balance between honoring the past while embracing the future is a lesson that resonates across industries, emphasizing the importance of respecting heritage while pursuing progress.

Sustainability as a Core Principle

In an era of increasing environmental awareness, Lee learned that sustainability must be a core principle in food innovation. Throughout his career, he witnessed the alarming rates of food waste and the environmental impact of industrial food production. This prompted him to explore sustainable practices, such as sourcing ingredients locally and minimizing packaging waste.

One of his notable initiatives involved partnering with local farmers to create a closed-loop system, where surplus produce was transformed into innovative food products. This not only reduced waste but also supported the local economy, demonstrating that sustainable practices can be both profitable and beneficial to the community. Lee's commitment to sustainability has inspired many in the culinary world to rethink their practices, proving that innovation can lead to a healthier planet.

The Importance of Continuous Learning

Lee's journey highlighted the necessity of continuous learning in an ever-evolving industry. The culinary and food technology landscape is constantly changing, with new techniques, ingredients, and consumer preferences emerging regularly. Lee embraced this by attending workshops, participating in food tech conferences, and engaging with emerging trends.

For instance, when plant-based diets surged in popularity, Lee committed to understanding the nutritional science behind plant-based ingredients, which allowed him to create products that were not only delicious but also nutritionally balanced. This commitment to lifelong learning has become a cornerstone of his philosophy, emphasizing that to remain relevant and innovative, one must always be willing to adapt and grow.

Cultivating Resilience and Adaptability

Finally, Lee learned the importance of resilience and adaptability in the face of challenges. The food industry is fraught with unpredictability, from shifting consumer trends to supply chain disruptions. During the COVID-19 pandemic, for example, Lee faced significant hurdles as restaurants closed and demand for certain products plummeted.

Rather than succumbing to despair, Lee pivoted his business model to focus on direct-to-consumer sales and meal kits, allowing Culinary Innovations Inc. to thrive despite the challenges. This experience underscored the lesson that adaptability is not just a survival tactic but a vital component of success in any entrepreneurial venture.

In conclusion, Lee Hernandez's culinary journey is a testament to the power of learning from experiences, both good and bad. By embracing failure, valuing collaboration, balancing tradition with innovation, prioritizing sustainability, committing to continuous learning, and cultivating resilience, Lee has not only transformed his career but has also left an indelible mark on the food technology landscape. His story serves as an inspiration for future generations of innovators, encouraging them to approach their journeys with curiosity, courage, and a commitment to making a difference.

Gratitude for the support and opportunities

In reflecting upon the remarkable journey of my culinary career, I find it imperative to express heartfelt gratitude for the myriad of supports and opportunities that have shaped my path. The culinary world is not merely a solitary endeavor; rather, it thrives on collaboration, mentorship, and the nurturing of relationships. Each experience has contributed to my growth as a culinary innovator, and it is essential to acknowledge the individuals and entities that have played pivotal roles in this journey.

First and foremost, I extend my deepest appreciation to my family, whose unwavering belief in my potential has been a cornerstone of my success. Growing up in a food-centric household, I was surrounded by the rich tapestry of culinary traditions that fostered my early love for cooking. My parents, who spent countless hours in the kitchen, instilled in me the values of hard work, creativity, and resilience. Their encouragement to pursue my passion for food technology has been invaluable. It is often said that behind every successful individual lies a supportive family, and in my case, this adage rings especially true.

Moreover, I am profoundly grateful to the mentors and educators who guided me through my culinary education. The Institute of Culinary Arts provided not only a rigorous academic curriculum but also an environment conducive to experimentation and growth. Professors who were not only experts in their fields but also passionate about nurturing young talent played a crucial role in my development. Their constructive feedback and encouragement allowed me to explore the boundaries of culinary science, particularly in the realm of molecular gastronomy. For instance, during my studies, I had the privilege of working on a project that involved the application of spherification techniques, which opened my eyes to the potential of food technology. This experience not only honed my technical skills but also ignited a passion for innovation that continues to drive my work today.

In addition to academic mentors, the culinary community has been a rich source of inspiration and support. Collaborating with renowned chefs and food scientists during my apprenticeship at Xperimental Foods Inc. was a transformative experience. The collaborative nature of the culinary field allowed me to engage in meaningful dialogues about food technology, leading to the creation of groundbreaking products like FlavorBurst™. The synergy created in such environments is essential for pushing the boundaries of culinary innovation. For example, brainstorming sessions with my colleagues often led to unexpected breakthroughs, such as the development of a new flavor extraction method that would not have been possible without their insights and expertise.

Furthermore, the support from industry professionals and investors has been instrumental in the success of Culinary Innovations Inc. Securing funding was not merely a financial transaction; it was a vote of confidence in my vision for the future of food technology. The trust placed in me by investors allowed me to assemble a talented team of culinary experts, each bringing unique perspectives and skills to the table. This diversity has been a driving force behind our ability to create products that resonate with consumers and meet the demands of an ever-evolving market.

As I reflect on the challenges faced along the way, it is evident that the journey has been fraught with obstacles. The culinary industry is competitive and often unforgiving, yet it is through the support of my network that I have navigated these challenges. From overcoming skepticism regarding new culinary techniques to managing the complexities of scaling a food tech startup, the encouragement from peers and mentors has been a source of strength. For instance, during a particularly challenging phase of product development, it was the advice and reassurance from my fellow entrepreneurs that helped me maintain focus and perseverance.

In conclusion, the gratitude I feel for the support and opportunities I have received is immeasurable. Each individual, from family members to mentors, colleagues, and industry partners, has contributed to my journey in profound ways. Their belief in my vision has fueled my passion for culinary innovation, and it is my hope that I can pay this support forward by mentoring the next generation of food innovators. As we continue to explore the future of food technology, I remain committed to fostering an environment where creativity, collaboration, and support thrive, ensuring that the culinary world remains a vibrant and dynamic space for all.

Inspiring future generations

Encouraging innovation and creativity

In the rapidly evolving world of culinary arts and food technology, fostering innovation and creativity is essential for progress and sustainability. Lee Hernandez's journey exemplifies how a blend of imagination, scientific inquiry, and culinary tradition can lead to groundbreaking advancements. This section explores the importance of innovation in the culinary field, the challenges faced by aspiring food technologists, and the strategies that can be employed to encourage creative thinking.

The Importance of Innovation in Culinary Arts

Innovation in culinary arts is not merely about creating new dishes; it encompasses a wide array of practices, including the development of novel cooking techniques, the use of technology to enhance food production, and the exploration of sustainable practices. As the global population continues to grow, the demand for food will increase, necessitating innovative solutions to ensure food security. According to the Food and Agriculture Organization (FAO), food production must increase by 70% by 2050 to meet the needs of the projected population of 9.7 billion people [?].

Challenges to Creativity

Despite the clear need for innovation, several challenges can stifle creativity in the culinary field:

+ **Conformity to Tradition:** Many chefs and culinary professionals may feel pressured to adhere to traditional cooking methods and recipes, which can limit experimentation. The fear of backlash from purists can deter chefs from exploring new ideas.

+ **Resource Limitations:** Access to high-quality ingredients, technology, and funding can be significant barriers for aspiring innovators. Without the necessary resources, it becomes challenging to test and implement new concepts.

+ **Market Resistance:** Consumers can be hesitant to embrace new flavors or techniques, leading to reluctance from chefs to introduce innovative dishes. This resistance can be rooted in cultural preferences or a lack of understanding of the benefits of innovation.

Strategies for Encouraging Innovation

To cultivate a culture of creativity in the culinary arts, several strategies can be implemented:

1. **Education and Training:** Culinary schools should incorporate courses that emphasize creativity and innovation. Programs that focus on molecular gastronomy, food science, and experimental cooking can empower students to think outside the box. For instance, the Institute of Culinary Arts has introduced workshops on flavor pairing and ingredient foraging, encouraging students to explore unconventional combinations.

2. **Collaboration and Networking:** Creating opportunities for collaboration among chefs, scientists, and food technologists can lead to innovative solutions. Networking events, hackathons, and culinary competitions can foster teamwork and inspire new ideas. Lee Hernandez's work at Xperimental Foods Inc. exemplifies the power of collaboration, where culinary experts and scientists united to push the boundaries of flavor and texture.

3. **Encouraging Risk-Taking:** Chefs should be encouraged to take risks in their culinary creations. Establishing an environment where failure is seen as a stepping stone to success can empower individuals to experiment without fear. For example, the "Fail Fast" philosophy adopted by many startups can be applied to culinary innovation, where chefs are encouraged to quickly prototype and test new dishes.

4. **Consumer Education:** Educating consumers about the benefits of innovative culinary practices can help reduce market resistance. Tasting events, cooking demonstrations, and social media campaigns can showcase the potential of new flavors and techniques, helping to shift consumer perceptions.

Examples of Successful Innovation

Several culinary innovators have successfully embraced creativity, leading to significant advancements in the industry:

+ **Ferrán Adrià:** Renowned for his avant-garde approach to cuisine, Adrià pioneered molecular gastronomy at his restaurant El Bulli. By deconstructing traditional dishes and utilizing scientific techniques, he created a new culinary language that has inspired countless chefs worldwide.

+ **Dan Barber:** A leader in sustainable cuisine, Barber emphasizes the importance of local and seasonal ingredients. His restaurant, Blue Hill at Stone Barns, showcases how innovation can align with sustainability, creating dishes that highlight the flavors of the region while promoting environmental stewardship.

+ **David Chang:** The founder of Momofuku, Chang has revolutionized modern Asian cuisine by blending traditional recipes with contemporary techniques. His willingness to experiment with flavors and textures has opened up new avenues for culinary creativity.

Conclusion

Encouraging innovation and creativity in the culinary arts is crucial for addressing the challenges of the future.   By fostering an environment that values experimentation, collaboration, and education, the next generation of food innovators can develop solutions that not only enhance culinary experiences but also contribute to a sustainable food system. Lee Hernandez's legacy serves as a reminder that with passion, creativity, and a willingness to embrace the unknown, the culinary world can continue to evolve and inspire.

Leaving a mark on culinary history

Lee Hernandez's journey through the culinary landscape has not only been a personal triumph but also a significant contribution to the evolution of food culture.   His innovations have reshaped how we perceive and experience food, leaving an indelible mark on culinary history. This section explores the theoretical implications of his work, the challenges he faced, and the examples of his lasting influence.

Theoretical Implications of Culinary Innovation

Culinary innovation, as exemplified by Hernandez, can be analyzed through the lens of several theoretical frameworks.   One such framework is the *Diffusion of Innovations Theory* proposed by Rogers (2003).   This theory explains how, why, and at what rate new ideas and technology spread.   Hernandez's FlavorBurst™ product serves as a case study in this context.   The product introduced a novel approach to flavor enhancement, characterized by its ability to alter perceptions of taste through molecular manipulation.

The formula for flavor perception can be modeled as:

$$P = f(F, T, A)$$

where P is perception, F represents flavor compounds, T is temperature, and A is aroma. Hernandez's work in food technology has effectively altered the variables in this equation, leading to a new understanding of how flavors can be enhanced and experienced.

Challenges in Culinary Innovation

Despite his successes, Hernandez faced numerous challenges that threatened to hinder his journey. One significant issue was the skepticism from traditional chefs and food critics. Many viewed his molecular gastronomy techniques as gimmicks rather than legitimate culinary advancements. This skepticism can be understood through the concept of *cultural resistance* to change, where established norms are upheld in the face of innovation.

To combat this resistance, Hernandez engaged in extensive outreach and education, demonstrating the scientific basis of his techniques through workshops and public demonstrations. By fostering dialogue between traditional and modern culinary practices, he bridged the gap between skepticism and acceptance.

Examples of Lasting Influence

Hernandez's impact on culinary history can be observed through various examples that illustrate his innovative spirit. One notable instance is his collaboration with local farmers to create sustainable food systems. By integrating technology with traditional farming practices, he not only enhanced the quality of ingredients but also promoted environmental stewardship. This approach aligns with the principles of *sustainable gastronomy*, which emphasizes the importance of sourcing ingredients responsibly.

Another example is the rise of fusion cuisine, which has become a hallmark of contemporary dining. Hernandez's ability to blend diverse culinary traditions has inspired countless chefs to experiment with flavors and techniques from around the world. This has led to the emergence of new dishes that reflect a global palate, thereby enriching the culinary landscape.

Inspiring Future Generations

The legacy of Lee Hernandez extends beyond his culinary creations; it encompasses his role as a mentor and advocate for aspiring chefs. By establishing scholarships and mentorship programs, he has actively contributed to the cultivation of the next generation of culinary innovators. His commitment to education underscores the importance of passing on knowledge and skills, ensuring that future chefs are equipped to navigate the evolving food industry.

Hernandez's influence is also evident in the increasing emphasis on food technology in culinary curricula. Educational institutions are now incorporating courses on molecular gastronomy and food science, reflecting the growing recognition of these fields as essential components of modern culinary education.

Conclusion

In conclusion, Lee Hernandez's journey is a testament to the power of innovation in shaping culinary history. Through his groundbreaking work, he has not only transformed the way we experience food but also established a framework for future culinary advancements. His legacy is one of inspiration, challenging aspiring chefs to think creatively and embrace the possibilities of culinary technology. As we look to the future, it is clear that Hernandez's contributions will continue to resonate within the culinary community, inspiring new generations to leave their own marks on this ever-evolving field.

Final thoughts and parting words

Appendix

Recipes inspired by Lee Hernandez's innovations

FlavorBurst™ creations

The FlavorBurst™ technology, pioneered by Lee Hernandez, represents a significant advancement in the field of food technology, merging culinary artistry with scientific precision. This section delves into the innovative creations that have emerged from this groundbreaking technique, exploring the underlying theory, practical applications, and the challenges faced during its development.

Theoretical Foundations

At its core, FlavorBurst™ is based on the principles of molecular gastronomy, which examines the physical and chemical transformations of ingredients that occur during cooking. The technology utilizes a combination of encapsulation techniques and flavor enhancement methods to create intense flavor experiences.

The fundamental equation governing the release of flavors in the FlavorBurst™ process can be expressed as follows:

$$F = \frac{C \cdot E}{T} \tag{77}$$

Where:

+ F = Flavor intensity

+ C = Concentration of flavor compounds

+ E = Efficiency of release mechanism

+ T = Time of exposure to heat or other stimuli

This equation highlights the delicate balance between concentration, efficiency, and time, which are critical for achieving the desired flavor profile in culinary creations.

Innovative Creations

1. FlavorBurst™ Pearls   One of the flagship products of the FlavorBurst™ line is the FlavorBurst™ Pearls.   These are small, caviar-like spheres that encapsulate intense flavors, allowing for a burst of taste upon consumption.   The process involves spherification, where a liquid containing concentrated flavors is dropped into a calcium bath, forming a gel-like membrane around the liquid center.

+ **Example:** *Citrus Burst Pearls* - These pearls encapsulate the essence of fresh citrus fruits, providing a refreshing explosion of flavor that can be used in salads, desserts, or as a garnish for cocktails.

2.   FlavorBurst™ Infusions   FlavorBurst™ Infusions are another innovative creation, where oils and liquids are infused with concentrated flavors using advanced extraction techniques. This method not only enhances the flavor but also preserves the integrity of the original ingredients.

+ **Example:** *Truffle-Infused Olive Oil* - By utilizing a cold extraction method, the rich aroma of truffles is captured in the oil, allowing chefs to elevate dishes with just a few drops.

3. FlavorBurst™ Dusts   FlavorBurst™ Dusts are dehydrated flavor concentrates that can be sprinkled onto dishes to add an intense flavor kick. This innovative product is created through a process of freeze-drying and grinding, ensuring that the essence of the original ingredient is preserved.

+ **Example:** *Smoked Paprika Dust* - This dust captures the smoky flavor of traditional paprika, providing a versatile seasoning for meats, vegetables, and even popcorn.

Challenges and Solutions

Despite the success of FlavorBurst™, the journey was not without its challenges. One of the primary issues faced was the skepticism from traditional chefs who were hesitant to embrace the technological advancements in culinary arts.   To address this, Lee Hernandez organized workshops and tastings, allowing chefs to experience the flavors firsthand and understand the science behind the creations.

Additionally, ensuring the consistency and quality of the FlavorBurst™ products was paramount. Rigorous testing and quality control measures were implemented, including:

+ Standardized flavor profiles through gas chromatography analysis.

+ Sensory evaluations conducted by panels of culinary experts to ensure the desired taste experience.

Conclusion

The FlavorBurst™ creations exemplify the fusion of culinary innovation and technology, showcasing how advancements can enhance the dining experience. By understanding the science behind flavor release and utilizing cutting-edge techniques, Lee Hernandez has not only transformed the way we perceive taste but has also inspired a new generation of chefs to explore the endless possibilities within the culinary landscape. The legacy of FlavorBurst™ will undoubtedly continue to shape the future of food technology, encouraging creativity and experimentation in kitchens around the world.

Molecular gastronomy experiments

Molecular gastronomy is an innovative field that merges the principles of food science with culinary arts, allowing chefs to explore the physical and chemical transformations of ingredients during cooking. This section delves into the theoretical foundation of molecular gastronomy, common challenges encountered, and illustrative examples of experiments that showcase its potential.

Theoretical Foundation

The core of molecular gastronomy lies in understanding the science behind cooking. It involves the manipulation of ingredients at a molecular level to create new textures, flavors, and presentations. Key concepts include:

+ **Emulsification:** This process involves mixing two immiscible liquids, such as oil and water, using an emulsifier like lecithin. The emulsifier reduces the surface tension between the liquids, allowing for a stable mixture. An example is the creation of a vinaigrette, where oil and vinegar are emulsified to form a cohesive dressing.

+ **Spherification:** This technique creates small spheres that burst with liquid when bitten into. It involves the use of sodium alginate and calcium chloride. The basic equation for the reaction is:

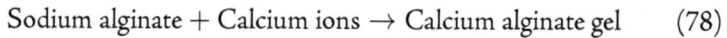

$$\text{Sodium alginate} + \text{Calcium ions} \rightarrow \text{Calcium alginate gel} \qquad (78)$$

This reaction occurs when a sodium alginate solution is dropped into a calcium chloride bath, forming a gel-like membrane around the liquid.

+ **Foaming:** Foams are created by incorporating air into a liquid using a stabilizing agent. The process can be enhanced using a whipping siphon. The equation for the formation of a foam can be represented as:

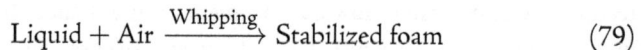

$$\text{Liquid} + \text{Air} \xrightarrow{\text{Whipping}} \text{Stabilized foam} \qquad (79)$$

Common stabilizers include gelatin or soy lecithin, which help maintain the structure of the foam.

+ **Gelification:** This process transforms liquids into gels using agents such as agar-agar or gelatin. The basic reaction can be expressed as:

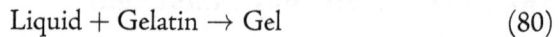

$$\text{Liquid} + \text{Gelatin} \rightarrow \text{Gel} \qquad (80)$$

The choice of gelling agent affects the texture and melting point of the final product.

Common Challenges

While molecular gastronomy offers exciting possibilities, it also presents several challenges:

+ **Ingredient Compatibility:** Not all ingredients work well together at a molecular level. Understanding the chemical properties of each ingredient is crucial for successful experimentation.

+ **Precision Required:** Many molecular gastronomy techniques require precise measurements and conditions. For instance, spherification must be performed at specific temperatures and concentrations to achieve the desired results.

+ **Equipment Needs:** Specialized equipment, such as sous-vide machines or whipping siphons, can be costly and may not be readily available in all kitchens.

+ **Consumer Acceptance:** Some diners may be hesitant to embrace unconventional textures and presentations, leading to challenges in menu development and marketing.

Illustrative Examples

To illustrate the principles of molecular gastronomy, consider the following experiments:

Experiment 1: Basic Spherification

+ **Ingredients:** 500 mL fruit juice, 5 g sodium alginate, 5 g calcium chloride, 500 mL water

+ **Procedure:**

    1. Mix sodium alginate with fruit juice using a blender until fully dissolved.
    2. Prepare a calcium chloride bath by dissolving calcium chloride in water.
    3. Using a syringe, drop the sodium alginate mixture into the calcium chloride bath to form spheres.
    4. Allow the spheres to set for 1-2 minutes before removing and rinsing in clean water.

+ **Result:** The spheres should have a gel-like exterior with liquid fruit juice inside, creating a burst of flavor when eaten.

Experiment 2: Creating a Fruit Foam

+ **Ingredients:** 200 mL fruit puree, 2 g soy lecithin, water

+ **Procedure:**

    1. Combine fruit puree and soy lecithin in a bowl.
    2. Use an immersion blender to whip the mixture until a stable foam forms.

3. Spoon the foam onto a dish as a garnish or serve alongside the fruit puree.

+ **Result:** A light and airy foam that enhances the presentation and flavor of the dish.

Experiment 3: Gelified Salad Dressing

+ **Ingredients:** 100 mL vinaigrette, 1 g agar-agar

+ **Procedure:**

1. Heat the vinaigrette in a saucepan and add agar-agar, stirring until dissolved.

2. Pour the mixture into a mold and refrigerate until set.

3. Unmold and serve as a gelled dressing on salads.

+ **Result:** A unique, gelled dressing that adds an interesting texture to salads.

Conclusion

Molecular gastronomy represents a frontier in culinary innovation, allowing chefs to experiment with the science of cooking to create extraordinary dining experiences. By understanding the theoretical principles, overcoming challenges, and engaging in creative experiments, culinary innovators like Lee Hernandez are shaping the future of food technology. The potential for new flavors, textures, and presentations continues to inspire chefs and food enthusiasts around the world, paving the way for a culinary revolution.

Sustainable and plant-based delights

In an era where environmental concerns are at the forefront of culinary innovation, sustainable and plant-based cuisine has emerged as a vital component of the future of food. The shift towards plant-based diets not only addresses health issues but also significantly reduces the ecological footprint associated with traditional animal farming. This section delves into the principles of sustainability within culinary practices, the challenges faced, and examples of innovative plant-based dishes that reflect Lee Hernandez's commitment to a greener future.

The Theory of Sustainability in Food

Sustainability in food systems refers to the ability to produce, process, and consume food in a manner that meets current needs without compromising the ability of future generations to meet theirs. This encompasses three primary pillars: environmental stewardship, economic viability, and social equity. The integration of these principles in culinary practices can lead to a more responsible and ethical food system.

$$\text{Sustainable Food System} = \text{Environmental Health} + \text{Economic Profitability} + \text{Social Equity} \tag{81}$$

Environmental Impact of Plant-Based Diets

The environmental impact of food choices is significant. Animal agriculture is a leading contributor to greenhouse gas emissions, deforestation, and water usage. According to the Food and Agriculture Organization (FAO), livestock production accounts for approximately 14.5% of global greenhouse gas emissions. In contrast, plant-based foods generally require fewer resources and produce lower emissions.

$$\text{GHG Emissions (kg CO}_2\text{e)} = (\text{Livestock Production}) + (\text{Plant Production}) \tag{82}$$

By substituting animal-based ingredients with plant-based alternatives, chefs can create dishes that are not only delicious but also environmentally friendly. For example, using lentils instead of beef can reduce the carbon footprint of a meal by up to 70%.

Challenges in Implementing Plant-Based Innovations

While the benefits of plant-based diets are clear, several challenges persist in their widespread adoption:

- **Cultural Resistance:** Many cultures have deeply rooted culinary traditions centered around meat consumption. Overcoming this resistance requires education and the introduction of flavorful plant-based alternatives.

- **Nutritional Concerns:** There is a perception that plant-based diets may lack essential nutrients, such as protein, iron, and vitamin B12. Innovative chefs must ensure that their dishes are nutritionally balanced.

+ **Accessibility and Affordability:** High-quality plant-based ingredients can be expensive and less accessible in certain regions, posing a barrier to adoption.

Innovative Plant-Based Dishes

Lee Hernandez's approach to sustainable cuisine is exemplified through his creations that prioritize both flavor and environmental responsibility. Below are a few notable examples:

+ **Mushroom and Quinoa Stuffed Peppers:** This dish features bell peppers filled with a savory mix of quinoa, mushrooms, and spices. Mushrooms are a sustainable protein source, requiring less water and land than traditional livestock.

+ **Cauliflower Steaks with Chimichurri Sauce:** Thick slices of cauliflower are grilled and served with a vibrant chimichurri made from fresh herbs. This dish showcases the versatility of vegetables while minimizing waste, as the entire cauliflower can be utilized.

+ **Chickpea and Sweet Potato Curry:** A hearty curry that combines chickpeas and sweet potatoes, offering a rich source of protein and fiber. This dish exemplifies the use of legumes and root vegetables, which are both sustainable and nutritious.

The Future of Sustainable Cuisine

As the culinary landscape evolves, the emphasis on sustainability and plant-based diets will continue to grow. The rise of food technology, such as lab-grown meat and plant-based meat alternatives, will further enhance the ability of chefs to create innovative dishes that appeal to a broader audience.

In conclusion, sustainable and plant-based delights represent a crucial aspect of the culinary innovations championed by Lee Hernandez. By embracing these principles, future chefs can not only contribute to a healthier planet but also inspire others to explore the diverse and flavorful world of plant-based cuisine.

Future Culinary Landscape = Innovation + Sustainability + Flavor   (83)

Resources for aspiring food technologists

Books, courses, and websites

In the rapidly evolving field of food technology, continuous learning and staying updated with the latest innovations is paramount. This section provides a curated list of essential books, online courses, and websites that aspiring food technologists can utilize to enhance their knowledge and skills.

Books

- **Molecular Gastronomy: Exploring the Science of Flavor** by Hervé This
  This foundational text dives into the scientific principles that underpin modern cooking techniques. Hervé This, a pioneer in molecular gastronomy, provides insights into how chemistry and physics can transform culinary practices. The book is filled with experiments and theoretical concepts that encourage readers to explore the science behind flavors.

- **The Flavor Bible** by Karen Page and Andrew Dornenburg
  This indispensable guide is a comprehensive resource for understanding flavor pairings. It offers a wealth of information on how different ingredients interact and provides suggestions for creating harmonious dishes. This book is essential for anyone looking to innovate in the kitchen by combining flavors in new and exciting ways.

- **On Food and Cooking: The Science and Lore of the Kitchen** by Harold McGee
  McGee's work is a classic reference that combines culinary history with scientific inquiry. It covers a broad range of topics, from the chemistry of cooking to the biology of ingredients. This book is perfect for those interested in the science behind food preparation and the transformative processes that occur during cooking.

- **Food Technology: Principles and Practice** by Paul D. E. Smith
  This textbook is an excellent resource for understanding the principles of food technology. It covers various topics, including food processing, preservation techniques, and quality control. The book is designed for students and professionals who wish to deepen their understanding of the food industry's technical aspects.

+ **Plant-Based Food Innovation for the Health and Sustainability Era** by Charis M. Galanakis
  This book focuses on the growing trend of plant-based diets and the innovations surrounding them. It discusses the nutritional benefits of plant-based foods, sustainable sourcing, and innovative processing techniques that enhance flavor and texture. A must-read for those interested in the future of food sustainability.

Courses

+ **Introduction to Food Technology** (Coursera)
  Offered by leading universities, this course provides an overview of food technology, covering topics such as food safety, preservation methods, and the impact of technology on food production. It's designed for beginners and provides a solid foundation for further study.

+ **Molecular Gastronomy: The Science of Cooking** (edX)
  This course focuses on the principles of molecular gastronomy, teaching students how to apply scientific techniques to create innovative dishes. It includes hands-on projects and encourages experimentation with flavors and textures.

+ **Plant-Based Cooking for Everyone** (Udemy)
  This course offers practical skills for creating delicious plant-based meals. It emphasizes the health benefits of plant-based diets and provides recipes that highlight innovative cooking techniques.

+ **Food Innovation and Product Development** (FutureLearn)
  This course is tailored for those interested in food product development. It covers the entire process from concept to market, including consumer trends, product testing, and branding strategies. Students will learn how to innovate within the food industry effectively.

+ **The Science of Gastronomy** (Hong Kong University of Science and Technology)
  This course explores the intersection of science and cooking, examining how different cooking methods affect flavor and texture. It includes experiments and discussions on the scientific principles behind culinary techniques.

Websites

+ **Food Technology Magazine**
  A leading publication that covers the latest trends and innovations in food technology. It features articles, research papers, and industry news that are valuable for professionals and enthusiasts alike.

+ **Institute of Food Technologists (IFT)**
  The IFT website offers a wealth of resources, including research articles, webinars, and networking opportunities for food technologists. It also provides access to professional development courses and certifications.

+ **Serious Eats**
  This website is an excellent resource for both culinary enthusiasts and professionals. It features in-depth articles, recipes, and cooking techniques that emphasize the science behind food preparation.

+ **The Food Lab**
  A section of Serious Eats, The Food Lab focuses on the science of cooking, providing insights into techniques and methods that enhance flavor and texture. It includes experiments and recipes that encourage innovation in the kitchen.

+ **Culinary Institute of America (CIA)**
  The CIA website offers information on culinary programs, workshops, and resources for aspiring chefs and food technologists. It includes articles on food trends, techniques, and industry news.

By utilizing these resources, aspiring food technologists can deepen their understanding of culinary innovation and stay ahead in the dynamic world of food technology. Whether through reading foundational texts, enrolling in specialized courses, or exploring online platforms, the journey of learning and discovery in this field is both exciting and essential for future innovators.

Organizations and events for food innovation

The landscape of food innovation is rich and diverse, comprising numerous organizations and events that foster creativity, collaboration, and technological advancements in the culinary world. These entities play a critical role in shaping the future of food by providing resources, networking opportunities, and platforms for sharing ideas. Below are some notable organizations and events that aspiring food technologists and innovators should consider engaging with.

Organizations

1. **The Institute of Food Technologists (IFT)**   Founded in 1939, the Institute of Food Technologists is a professional organization dedicated to advancing the science of food. IFT provides a wealth of resources including journals, conferences, and networking opportunities that connect food scientists, technologists, and industry professionals. The organization's annual meeting, known as the IFT Annual Event and Food Expo, showcases the latest innovations in food technology and research, offering a platform for professionals to exchange ideas and collaborate on new projects.

2. **Food Innovation Network (FIN)**   The Food Innovation Network is a collaborative initiative that connects food entrepreneurs, researchers, and industry experts to drive innovation in the food sector. FIN provides access to resources such as funding opportunities, workshops, and mentorship programs. Through its network, members can collaborate on projects that address pressing challenges in the food industry, including sustainability and health.

3. **The Food and Agriculture Organization (FAO)**   As a specialized agency of the United Nations, the FAO plays a pivotal role in addressing global food security and sustainability issues. The organization conducts research and provides guidelines that influence food policy and innovation worldwide. Their initiatives often focus on integrating technology into agriculture and food production, promoting sustainable practices that can be adopted by innovators in the food sector.

4. **The Culinary Institute of America (CIA)**   The Culinary Institute of America is renowned for its culinary education and innovation programs. CIA not only trains the next generation of chefs but also focuses on food technology and sustainability. The institute hosts events such as the Worlds of Flavor International Conference and Festival, which brings together chefs, food professionals, and innovators to explore global food trends and technologies.

Events

1. **Food Tech Summit**   The Food Tech Summit is an annual event that brings together startups, investors, and industry leaders to discuss the future of food technology. The summit features keynote speakers, panel discussions, and networking opportunities, allowing participants to explore emerging trends and

technologies in food innovation. Topics often include plant-based alternatives, food safety, and sustainable production methods.

2. SIAL Paris SIAL Paris is one of the largest food innovation exhibitions in the world, showcasing new products and trends in the food industry. Held every two years, the event attracts thousands of exhibitors and visitors from around the globe. SIAL serves as a platform for food innovators to present their latest creations, explore market opportunities, and network with industry professionals.

3. The Future of Food Tech Conference This conference focuses on the intersection of technology and food, highlighting innovations that are transforming the industry. Attendees can expect discussions on topics such as artificial intelligence in food production, blockchain for supply chain transparency, and the role of data analytics in food safety. The event fosters collaboration between tech entrepreneurs and food industry leaders, encouraging the development of groundbreaking solutions.

4. Expo West Natural Products Expo West is a premier event for the natural, organic, and healthy products industry, including food innovation. The expo features thousands of exhibitors showcasing their latest products, along with educational sessions and networking opportunities. This event is an excellent venue for food innovators to discover new trends, connect with potential partners, and gain insights into consumer preferences.

5. The Good Food Conference Organized by the Good Food Institute, this conference focuses on promoting plant-based and cultivated meat innovations. The event gathers entrepreneurs, scientists, and advocates to discuss strategies for scaling up alternative protein sources. Attendees can engage in workshops, hear from industry leaders, and learn about the latest research and developments in sustainable food technology.

Conclusion

Engaging with these organizations and events can significantly enhance the knowledge and skills of aspiring food technologists. By participating in workshops, networking with industry professionals, and staying informed about the latest trends, innovators can contribute to the evolution of the food industry. Whether through collaboration, research, or entrepreneurship, the opportunities for making a meaningful impact in food innovation are vast and varied. By leveraging the resources provided by these organizations and events, the next generation of food innovators can help shape a sustainable and delicious future for all.

Continuing the legacy of Lee Hernandez's work

The impact of Lee Hernandez on the culinary world extends far beyond his innovative products and successful ventures. His legacy is characterized by a commitment to sustainability, education, and the continuous evolution of food technology. As aspiring food technologists and innovators seek to build upon his achievements, several key areas emerge as focal points for continuing his work.

Education and Mentorship

One of the most effective ways to honor Lee's legacy is through education and mentorship. By establishing scholarships and programs for aspiring chefs and food technologists, Lee has paved the way for the next generation. Educational institutions can develop curricula that emphasize the importance of both culinary arts and food science, integrating hands-on experiences with theoretical knowledge.

For instance, the incorporation of molecular gastronomy into culinary programs not only enhances students' understanding of flavor and texture but also encourages experimentation. As Lee often stated, "Innovation is born from curiosity." Therefore, fostering an environment that encourages questions and creative thinking is crucial.

Sustainability in Food Production

Another critical aspect of continuing Lee Hernandez's legacy involves the commitment to sustainability. The modern food industry faces significant challenges, including climate change, resource depletion, and food waste. Lee's work emphasized the importance of sustainable practices, such as sourcing local ingredients and reducing waste through innovative solutions.

To further this aspect of his legacy, food technologists can explore methods such as:

$$\text{Sustainable Yield} = \frac{\text{Total Output}}{\text{Input}} \times 100 \tag{84}$$

This equation can help assess the efficiency of food production systems. By maximizing sustainable yield, innovators can contribute to a more resilient food system. For example, implementing vertical farming techniques can significantly reduce land use and water consumption while increasing food production in urban areas.

Collaboration Across Disciplines

Lee's success was also rooted in his ability to collaborate with scientists, chefs, and entrepreneurs. Continuing his legacy requires fostering interdisciplinary collaborations that bring together diverse perspectives and expertise. By working with agricultural scientists, nutritionists, and environmentalists, food technologists can develop holistic solutions that address complex food system challenges.

For instance, the development of plant-based alternatives to traditional animal products has gained momentum in recent years. Collaborative efforts between food technologists and agricultural scientists can lead to breakthroughs in flavor and texture that satisfy consumer demand while promoting sustainability.

Technological Advancements

The rapid advancement of technology presents numerous opportunities to build on Lee's innovations. Emerging technologies such as artificial intelligence, machine learning, and biotechnology can revolutionize food production and distribution. For example, AI can optimize supply chain logistics, reducing food waste and improving efficiency.

Moreover, biotechnology can enhance food safety and nutritional content. Innovations like CRISPR gene editing allow for the development of crops that are more resistant to pests and diseases, ultimately leading to higher yields and reduced reliance on chemical pesticides.

Global Challenges and Food Security

As the world grapples with issues of food security, Lee's legacy encourages food innovators to address these challenges head-on. With an ever-growing population, it is imperative to develop sustainable and efficient food systems that can meet global demands.

Innovators can take inspiration from Lee's work by focusing on local solutions that are adaptable to various cultural contexts. For example, developing community-based food systems that empower local farmers and promote biodiversity can help ensure food security while honoring traditional practices.

Inspiring Future Generations

Finally, continuing Lee Hernandez's legacy involves inspiring future generations to embrace innovation and creativity in the culinary arts. By sharing stories of his journey, challenges, and triumphs, educators and industry leaders can motivate young individuals to pursue their passions fearlessly.

Encouraging participation in culinary competitions, innovation challenges, and community projects can ignite the spark of creativity in aspiring food technologists. As Lee once said, "Every great dish starts with a single idea." By nurturing that idea, we can cultivate a new wave of culinary innovators ready to make their mark on the world.

In conclusion, the legacy of Lee Hernandez is not merely a reflection of his achievements but a call to action for those who follow in his footsteps. By prioritizing education, sustainability, collaboration, technological advancement, and inspiration, we can ensure that his impact on the culinary world endures for generations to come.

Acknowledgments

Gratitude to the individuals who supported the project

Friends, family, and colleagues

The journey of Lee Hernandez in the world of culinary innovation would not have been possible without the unwavering support and encouragement from his friends, family, and colleagues. Each of these groups played a pivotal role in shaping his career and fostering his passion for food technology.

Family Support

Lee was born into a food-centric family, where culinary traditions were not just a part of life but a way of bonding. His parents, both avid cooks, instilled in him the values of creativity and experimentation in the kitchen. Family gatherings often revolved around cooking, where recipes were exchanged, and new dishes were born. This familial support laid the foundation for Lee's culinary journey.

> "Cooking was our family language. We expressed love through flavors and shared experiences through meals."

This nurturing environment allowed Lee to experiment freely with ingredients, leading to his early signs of culinary talent. His family encouraged him to pursue his passion, which ultimately led to his enrollment at the prestigious Institute of Culinary Arts.

Friendship and Collaboration

Throughout his educational and professional journey, Lee formed lifelong friendships with fellow culinary students and professionals. These friendships were not merely social; they became collaborative partnerships that enriched his learning experience.

One notable example is his friendship with Alex, a fellow student who shared Lee's passion for molecular gastronomy. Together, they conducted experiments that pushed the boundaries of traditional cooking. Their collaboration resulted in innovative techniques that would later influence Lee's product development at Culinary Innovations Inc.

$$\text{Innovation} = \text{Creativity} + \text{Collaboration} \qquad (85)$$

This equation illustrates the synergy that arises when creative minds come together. Lee and Alex's partnership exemplified how collaborative efforts can lead to groundbreaking culinary techniques and products.

Professional Mentorship

In the professional realm, Lee was fortunate to have mentors who guided him through the complexities of the food technology industry. Notably, his apprenticeship at Xperimental Foods Inc. introduced him to renowned scientists and industry experts. One mentor, Dr. Sarah Thompson, was instrumental in Lee's understanding of the scientific principles behind food technology.

Dr. Thompson often emphasized the importance of resilience in the face of skepticism. She taught Lee that innovation often meets resistance and that persistence is key to overcoming challenges. Her mentorship not only provided Lee with technical knowledge but also instilled in him the confidence to pursue his vision for FlavorBurst™.

> "Every great innovation faces skepticism. It's the visionaries who persevere that change the world."

Community and Networking

Lee's journey was also supported by a broader community of culinary professionals and innovators. Industry events, workshops, and conferences provided networking opportunities that were crucial for his entrepreneurial ventures. These gatherings allowed Lee to connect with investors, suppliers, and fellow innovators who shared his passion for transforming the food industry.

For instance, at the annual Food Tech Summit, Lee met several key investors who would later support his startup, Culinary Innovations Inc. The relationships he built at such events were fundamental in securing the resources necessary for his entrepreneurial success.

Conclusion

In conclusion, the contributions of friends, family, and colleagues were vital to Lee Hernandez's journey as a culinary innovator. Their support, collaboration, and mentorship provided the foundation upon which he built his career. As Lee often reflects, the path to innovation is rarely a solitary one; it is paved with the encouragement and inspiration of those who believe in you.

"I owe my success to the people who stood by me, challenged me, and believed in my vision."

Culinary experts and researchers

In the realm of food technology and innovation, the contributions of culinary experts and researchers are invaluable. These professionals not only advance the science of cooking but also bridge the gap between culinary arts and food science, leading to groundbreaking discoveries that enhance our understanding of food and its impact on health, sustainability, and culture. This section aims to acknowledge their pivotal roles and explore the theoretical frameworks, prevalent challenges, and notable examples that underscore their influence in the culinary field.

Theoretical Frameworks

Culinary experts and researchers operate within a variety of theoretical frameworks that guide their work. One prominent theory is the **Flavor Pairing Theory**, which posits that certain foods share common flavor compounds, leading to enhanced taste experiences when combined. This concept is grounded in the science of chemistry and sensory perception, suggesting that the molecular composition of foods can predict successful flavor combinations. For example, the pairing of strawberries and basil is supported by their shared volatile compounds, which can create a harmonious dish.

Another relevant framework is the **Molecular Gastronomy Theory**, which investigates the physical and chemical transformations of ingredients during cooking. This field employs scientific methods to explore how cooking techniques affect flavor, texture, and aroma. Notable researchers such as Hervé This and Ferran Adrià have pioneered this approach, leading to innovations like spherification and foaming, which have transformed traditional culinary practices.

Challenges in Culinary Research

Despite the advancements made by culinary experts and researchers, several challenges persist in the field. One major issue is the **replication of results**. Culinary experiments often yield subjective results based on individual taste preferences, making it difficult to achieve consistent outcomes. This variability can hinder the development of standardized recipes and food products.

Another challenge is the **integration of technology in traditional cooking**. While technology offers new methods and tools for food preparation, it can also lead to resistance from traditional chefs who may view these innovations as a threat to their craft. Balancing the art of cooking with scientific advancements requires careful consideration and open-mindedness from both chefs and researchers.

Notable Examples of Culinary Innovation

The contributions of culinary experts and researchers have led to numerous innovations that have significantly impacted the food industry. One notable example is the work of Chef Heston Blumenthal, who has embraced molecular gastronomy to create unique dining experiences. His dish, *Sound of the Sea*, incorporates edible sand and a seashell that plays ocean sounds, stimulating multiple senses and enhancing the overall experience of the meal.

Another example is the research conducted at the **University of California, Davis**, where scientists have developed new techniques for enhancing the flavor and shelf life of fruits and vegetables through controlled ripening processes. This research has implications for reducing food waste and improving the nutritional quality of produce available to consumers.

Furthermore, the collaboration between culinary experts and food scientists has led to the development of plant-based alternatives that mimic the taste and texture of meat. Companies like **Impossible Foods** and **Beyond Meat** have utilized research in flavor chemistry and plant protein structure to create products that appeal to both vegetarians and meat-lovers alike. These innovations not only cater to changing consumer preferences but also address environmental concerns associated with meat production.

Conclusion

The contributions of culinary experts and researchers are essential for the evolution of the food industry. Their work not only enhances our understanding of flavor and cooking techniques but also addresses pressing challenges such as sustainability, food waste, and health. As we continue to explore the future of food technology, the collaboration between culinary arts and scientific research will remain crucial in shaping a more innovative and sustainable food landscape. Acknowledging their efforts is vital, as it inspires future generations to push the boundaries of culinary innovation and create a lasting impact on the world of food.

Bibliography

[1] Blumenthal, H. (2004). *The Fat Duck Cookbook*. Bloomsbury Publishing.

[2] This, H. (2006). *Molecular Gastronomy: Exploring the Science of Flavor*. Columbia University Press.

[3] University of California, Davis. (2020). *Innovations in Food Science: Improving Flavor and Shelf Life of Produce*. Retrieved from `https://ucdavis.edu/food-science-innovations`

[4] Impossible Foods. (2021). *How It Works*. Retrieved from `https://impossiblefoods.com/how-it-works`

[5] Beyond Meat. (2021). *Our Products*. Retrieved from `https://www.beyondmeat.com/products`

Industry professionals and partners

In the realm of culinary innovation, collaboration with industry professionals and partners is essential for success. Lee Hernandez's journey is a testament to the power of these relationships, which not only foster creativity but also bridge the gap between traditional culinary arts and cutting-edge food technology.

The Role of Industry Professionals

Industry professionals, including chefs, food scientists, nutritionists, and business strategists, play a pivotal role in shaping the landscape of food technology. Their diverse expertise contributes to the development of innovative products that meet the evolving demands of consumers. For instance, Lee's collaboration with food scientists at Xperimental Foods Inc. allowed him to explore the molecular structure of flavor compounds, leading to the creation of FlavorBurst™.

Flavor Profile $= f$(Molecular Structure, Cooking Technique, Ingredient Quality)
$$(86)$$
This equation illustrates how various factors contribute to the overall flavor profile of a dish, emphasizing the importance of interdisciplinary collaboration.

Building Partnerships

Successful partnerships are built on shared values and goals. Lee Hernandez sought out partnerships with local farmers, suppliers, and sustainability experts to ensure that his products not only tasted great but also supported ethical practices. For example, his commitment to reducing food waste led him to collaborate with farmers to source imperfect produce that would otherwise go to waste, transforming it into high-quality ingredients for his FlavorBurst™ line.

Challenges in Collaboration

While collaboration has many benefits, it also presents challenges. Differing perspectives and priorities can lead to conflicts. For instance, when developing a new plant-based product, Lee faced disagreements with a partner who prioritized cost over sustainability. This conflict highlighted the need for clear communication and a shared vision. By facilitating open discussions and focusing on their common goal of creating innovative, sustainable food products, they were able to realign their efforts and successfully launch a new line of environmentally friendly snacks.

Examples of Successful Collaborations

Several successful collaborations in the culinary industry serve as examples of the potential that industry partnerships hold. One notable case is the partnership between renowned chef José Andrés and the World Central Kitchen, which focuses on providing meals in the wake of disasters. This collaboration demonstrates how culinary expertise can be leveraged for social good, inspiring others in the industry to think beyond profit and consider their impact on communities.

Similarly, Lee's collaboration with nutritionists led to the development of FlavorBurst™ products that cater to specific dietary needs, such as gluten-free and low-sodium options. This partnership not only expanded his product line but also ensured that consumers with dietary restrictions could enjoy delicious and innovative food.

Networking and Community Engagement

Engaging with industry professionals extends beyond formal partnerships. Networking events, culinary competitions, and industry conferences provide opportunities for chefs and food technologists to share ideas, learn from one another, and foster collaborations. Lee often participates in such events, where he connects with like-minded innovators and establishes relationships that can lead to future projects.

For instance, at the annual Food Tech Summit, Lee met a group of young entrepreneurs passionate about sustainable food practices. This encounter led to a collaborative project that focused on developing plant-based alternatives to traditional dairy products, showcasing how networking can ignite new ideas and ventures.

Conclusion

The importance of industry professionals and partners in the culinary world cannot be overstated. Their contributions to innovation, sustainability, and community engagement are vital for the future of food technology. By fostering strong relationships and navigating the challenges of collaboration, Lee Hernandez has not only advanced his career but has also made a significant impact on the culinary landscape. As the industry continues to evolve, the partnerships formed today will shape the future of food and inspire the next generation of culinary innovators.

About the Author

Mei Moreno's passion for food and innovation

Inspiration behind writing Culinary Futures

The inspiration behind writing *Culinary Futures* stems from a profound fascination with the intersection of food, technology, and culture. As a food journalist and researcher, I have always been captivated by how culinary innovations shape our eating habits, influence societal norms, and address pressing global challenges. The rapid advancements in food technology present both exciting opportunities and complex dilemmas that require careful exploration and understanding.

In recent years, the food industry has witnessed a surge of technological innovations aimed at enhancing food production, improving sustainability, and catering to diverse dietary needs. This transformation is not merely a trend; it reflects a fundamental shift in how we perceive food and its role in our lives. With the world facing issues such as climate change, food insecurity, and health crises, the need for innovative solutions has never been more critical.

One of the primary motivations for writing this book was to highlight the potential of culinary innovators like Lee Hernandez, who embody the spirit of creativity and resilience in the face of challenges. Through his journey, I aim to illustrate how individuals can leverage technology to create meaningful change in the food industry. Hernandez's pioneering work in food technology exemplifies the delicate balance between culinary artistry and scientific exploration. His creation of FlavorBurst™, a revolutionary food product that unlocks new taste sensations, is a testament to the power of innovation in transforming our culinary experiences.

Moreover, the book seeks to address the theoretical frameworks that underpin food technology and innovation. Drawing from various disciplines, including gastronomy, food science, and entrepreneurship, I explore how these fields converge to foster an environment ripe for creativity. For instance, the principles of molecular gastronomy, which combine culinary arts with scientific techniques, provide a rich context for understanding how food can be reimagined. This approach not only enhances flavors but also challenges traditional notions of cooking and eating.

An essential aspect of this exploration is the acknowledgment of the problems that accompany rapid technological advancements. While innovations such as lab-grown meat and plant-based alternatives offer promising solutions to environmental concerns, they also raise ethical questions about food production and consumption. How do we ensure that these technologies are accessible and equitable? What are the implications for small-scale farmers and traditional food producers? These questions are critical as we navigate the future of food.

In writing *Culinary Futures*, I sought to provide a balanced perspective that considers both the potential and the pitfalls of food technology. The narrative of Lee Hernandez serves as a lens through which readers can engage with these issues, inspiring them to think critically about the food choices they make and the impact of those choices on the world around them. By sharing his story, I hope to ignite a passion for innovation in aspiring chefs and food technologists, encouraging them to explore new frontiers in the culinary arts.

Ultimately, my goal is to inspire future generations to embrace creativity and innovation in their culinary pursuits. The journey of Lee Hernandez is not just about personal success; it is about a collective movement towards a more sustainable and inclusive food system. By documenting this journey, I aim to contribute to the ongoing dialogue about the future of food, highlighting the importance of collaboration, sustainability, and ethical considerations in shaping a better world through culinary innovation.

In conclusion, the inspiration behind *Culinary Futures* is deeply rooted in a desire to explore and celebrate the transformative power of food technology. By examining the life and achievements of Lee Hernandez, I hope to provide readers with insights and inspiration that will encourage them to engage with the future of food in meaningful ways. As we stand on the brink of a culinary revolution, it is essential to recognize the potential for innovation to not only enhance our gastronomic experiences but also to address the pressing challenges of our time.

Background in food journalism and research

Mei Moreno's journey into the realm of food journalism and research began with a deep-rooted passion for culinary arts and an insatiable curiosity about the science behind food. With a Bachelor's degree in Food Science from the University of Gastronomy, she developed a strong foundation in both the technical and creative aspects of food. This academic background provided her with the necessary tools to explore the multifaceted world of food, encompassing everything from nutrition to gastronomy.

During her time at university, Mei was particularly fascinated by the intersection of food and technology. She delved into the emerging field of food technology, studying how innovations such as molecular gastronomy and food preservation techniques could reshape culinary practices. This academic exploration was not merely theoretical; it was complemented by hands-on experiences in various kitchens, where she applied her knowledge to create dishes that were both innovative and delicious.

Theoretical Framework

In her research, Mei often referenced the theory of *Culinary Innovation*, which posits that the evolution of cuisine is driven by a combination of cultural influences, technological advancements, and consumer preferences. This theory can be summarized by the equation:

$$C = f(T, C_i, P)$$

Where: - C represents culinary innovation, - T denotes technological advancements, - C_i symbolizes cultural influences, and - P refers to consumer preferences.

This equation illustrates that culinary innovation is a function of these three variables. For instance, the rise of plant-based diets has prompted chefs to experiment with new ingredients and techniques, leading to the creation of innovative dishes that cater to changing consumer demands.

Challenges in Food Journalism

As Mei transitioned into food journalism, she encountered several challenges that shaped her perspective on the industry. One significant issue was the prevalence of misinformation surrounding food trends. In an era where social media amplifies voices, distinguishing between credible sources and sensationalized claims became increasingly difficult. Mei emphasized the importance of evidence-based reporting, advocating for a journalistic approach that prioritizes scientific research and expert opinions over anecdotal evidence.

In her articles, Mei often tackled contentious topics such as the health implications of genetically modified organisms (GMOs) and the sustainability of certain food practices. For example, she conducted an in-depth investigation into the environmental impact of factory farming versus regenerative agriculture, highlighting the need for sustainable practices in food production. Her findings underscored the complexity of these issues, revealing that simplistic narratives often fail to capture the nuances of food systems.

Examples of Research Contributions

Mei's contributions to food journalism are exemplified through her feature articles in prominent culinary magazines and online platforms. One notable piece titled "The Future of Food: Balancing Innovation and Tradition" explored the delicate balance between embracing new technologies and preserving culinary heritage. In this article, she interviewed chefs who are at the forefront of culinary innovation, showcasing how they incorporate traditional techniques into modern practices.

Additionally, Mei's research on food waste led to the publication of a groundbreaking report, "Waste Not: The Economic and Environmental Costs of Food Waste." This report provided statistical insights into the staggering amounts of food wasted globally, estimated at approximately 1.3 billion tons annually, according to the Food and Agriculture Organization (FAO). Mei's work highlighted innovative solutions adopted by restaurants and food businesses to mitigate waste, such as upcycling ingredients and implementing more efficient inventory management systems.

Conclusion

In summary, Mei Moreno's background in food journalism and research is characterized by a commitment to uncovering the truth behind culinary practices and innovations. Her academic training, coupled with her hands-on experiences in the kitchen, has equipped her with a unique perspective that she brings to her writing. By addressing the challenges of misinformation and advocating for sustainable practices, Mei aims to inspire a new generation of food enthusiasts and innovators. Her work not only informs the public but also contributes to the ongoing dialogue about the future of food in an ever-evolving landscape.

Future projects and endeavors

As I continue my journey as a food journalist and researcher, I am excited to explore several innovative projects that align with my passion for culinary arts and technology. My future endeavors will focus on three primary areas: sustainable food practices, the integration of technology in culinary education, and the promotion of food equity.

Sustainable Food Practices

The urgency of addressing climate change and its impact on food systems has never been more critical. One of my upcoming projects involves collaborating with local farmers and food producers to develop sustainable practices that can be adopted across various agricultural sectors. This initiative aims to reduce carbon footprints while enhancing food quality and availability.

Theory and Approach The concept of sustainable food systems is grounded in the principles of ecological balance and social equity. According to the *Food and Agriculture Organization (FAO)*, sustainable agriculture must meet the needs of the present without compromising the ability of future generations to meet their own needs. This involves a multi-faceted approach that includes:

+ **Crop Rotation:** Implementing crop rotation can improve soil health and reduce pest infestations. For example, rotating legumes with cereal crops enriches the soil with nitrogen, leading to healthier harvests.

+ **Water Conservation:** Techniques such as drip irrigation minimize water waste and ensure that crops receive adequate hydration. Research indicates that drip irrigation can increase crop yields by up to 90% compared to traditional methods.

+ **Organic Practices:** Encouraging organic farming reduces reliance on synthetic fertilizers and pesticides, promoting biodiversity and healthier ecosystems.

Integration of Technology in Culinary Education

Another project I am passionate about is the integration of technology into culinary education. With the rise of digital platforms and online learning, I plan to develop a series of interactive workshops and courses that leverage technology to enhance the learning experience for aspiring chefs.

Challenges and Solutions One of the primary challenges in culinary education is ensuring that students receive hands-on experience while also understanding the theoretical aspects of food science. To address this, I propose the following strategies:

+ **Virtual Reality (VR) Experiences:** Utilizing VR technology can simulate kitchen environments, allowing students to practice techniques in a safe and controlled setting. Studies have shown that VR training can improve skill retention by up to 75%.

+ **Online Collaboration Platforms:** Creating a platform where students can collaborate on projects, share recipes, and provide feedback can foster a sense of community and enhance learning outcomes.

+ **Interactive Recipe Development:** Incorporating software that allows students to experiment with flavor profiles and ingredient substitutions can encourage creativity and innovation in recipe development.

Promotion of Food Equity

Food equity is a pressing issue that affects millions globally. My future endeavors will also focus on advocating for food justice and accessibility, ensuring that all communities have access to nutritious food.

Theoretical Framework The theory of food sovereignty, as proposed by the *Nyéléni Declaration*, emphasizes the right of peoples to healthy and culturally appropriate food produced through ecologically sound and sustainable methods. This framework will guide my efforts in promoting food equity through the following initiatives:

+ **Community Gardens:** Establishing community gardens in urban areas can empower residents to grow their own food, fostering a sense of ownership and connection to their food sources.

+ **Food Literacy Programs:** Developing educational programs that teach individuals about nutrition, cooking skills, and the importance of local food systems can help combat food insecurity.

+ **Partnerships with Nonprofits:** Collaborating with organizations dedicated to food justice can amplify efforts to address systemic barriers to food access, providing resources and support to underserved communities.

Conclusion

In conclusion, my future projects and endeavors will focus on creating a more sustainable, equitable, and innovative food system. By integrating technology into culinary education, advocating for sustainable practices, and promoting food equity, I hope to inspire the next generation of food innovators. These projects not only reflect my passion for food but also my commitment to making a positive impact on the culinary landscape. As I embark on these endeavors, I look forward to sharing my journey and the lessons learned along the way with readers and aspiring culinary professionals alike.

Index

Milton Keynes UK
Ingram Content Group UK Ltd.
UKHW030743121124
451094UK00013B/1010

9 781779 666123